THE THIRD TOWER OF BABEL

The Solution...
To a Five Thousand Year Mystery Involving
the Ark of the Covenant, Ancient Egypt, and
the Second Coming of Jesus Christ

Stephen Banks

Dedication

This book is dedicated:

To the people of the Old and New Covenants, and for those curious enough to seek the meaning behind both. May these truths help enlighten the path which lies ahead, in times of plenty and in times of want.

To those who supported the writing of this book, and who encouraged the author through the fog of seemingly endless research.

And to the Holy Spirit who is the Revealer of all mysteries and the Giver of all true wisdom.

Isa 45:2-3

I will go before you and will level the mountains; I will break down gates of bronze and cut through bars of iron. I will give you the treasures of darkness, riches stored in secret places, so that you may know that I am the LORD, the God of Israel, who summons you by name.

Acknowledgements

My thanks to those who aided in the collection of the material and research for this book, and who generously provided ideas and illustrations, including: Bill Banks, the staff at Impact Books, the staff at the Wyatt Museum, Kersti Levy, Cindy Getchman, Tim Bode, Scott Ward and his missionary team in Africa. Thanks also to the staffs at the following libraries: the British Museum in London, and the Judiska Biblioteket in Stockholm.

TABLE OF CONTENTS

ILLUSTRATIONS

Page 67 - "Kidron Valley: Tomb of Zechariah" Image courtesy of HolyLandPhotos.org, <http://www.HolyLandPhotos.org> © 2002

Page 81 - "The Ziggurat of Nabonidus Restored" Sometric Projection. Drawing by Marjorie V. Duffell, 1937. Courtesy of the University of Pennsylvania Museum. Originally appeared in *The Ziggurat and its Surroundings* by Leonard Woolley, London: Oxford University Press, © 1939. Publication of the Joint Expedition of the British Museum and of the University Museum, University of Pennsylvania, Philadelphia to Mesopotamia: Ur Excavations; V.5., Plate #88.

Page 98, 109, 168 - "The Ark Of The Covenant," courtesy of Wyatt Archeological Research and the Wyatt Museum, <http://www.wyattmuseum.com> © 1995

Page 112 - The cover of *På Rätta Vägar*, Johan Millén. Courtesy of the Judiska Biblioteket in Stockholm.

All other illustrations are from the author's own collection.

PREFACE

There are images of the Messiah with which we have a degree of comfort. These have been provided in Scripture as a means of revealing specific aspects of His nature and His work. He is described, for instance, as the sacrificial Passover Lamb that came to take away the sins of the world (John 1:29). He is also described as a Root or Branch from which the future children and lineage of God would arise (Rom. 11:16). He is referred to as the Vine, and those who are joined to Him through the Holy Spirit draw from His source of life, and bear fruit in His Father's kingdom (John 15:1).

There are, however, other images of the Messiah that remain unexplored. One example is found in the Book of Revelation.

Rev 5:6
"Then I saw a Lamb, looking as if it had been slain, standing in the center of the throne...He had seven horns and **seven eyes, which are the seven spirits of God sent out into all the earth."**

Here, the Messiah is presented as a Lamb that had been slain, *with seven eyes*. Most would agree that this is not a familiar image of the Messiah; it is most certainly not an image that first comes to mind. Such descriptive imagery encourages us to ask questions, such as: Why are there seven eyes? And, are these eyes somehow related to the fact that the Lamb has been slain? Clearly, there are images of the Messiah that need further explanation.

There is, in fact, another image of the Messiah – one that has lain dormant for more than 2,500 years. While this image is mentioned repeatedly in Scripture, it has been largely overlooked. Yet, this specific portrayal of Jesus Christ reveals one of the most important messages for the end-time Church, and announces the coming reign of the Messiah as King on earth. This image is the Messiah as the living Stone, otherwise mysteriously referred to as the *capstone*.

As we will see, the appearance of this stone coincides with some of the most significant prophecies in the Bible. Furthermore, this stone's relevance spans the entire history of mankind, and is tied integrally to man's destiny.

Stephen Banks
November 2002

PART I

INTRODUCTION TO THE MYSTERY

1

THE CENTER OF ALL PROPHECY

Zechariah the prophet is a man of few words. Within a short list of chapters, he introduces some of the most comprehensive themes regarding the first and second comings of the Messiah. In the midst of the pages of his book, he creates an axis for the rest of Biblical prophecy. This occurs in the fourth chapter. Here, the prophet provides an incredible overview of the completed history of mankind.

ZECHARIAH 4

6 So he said to me, "This is the word of the LORD to Zerubbabel: 'Not by might nor by power, but by my Spirit,' says the LORD Almighty.

7 "What are you, O mighty mountain? Before Zerubbabel you will become level ground. Then he will bring out the capstone to shouts of 'God bless it! God bless it!'"

8 Then the word of the LORD came to me:

9 "The hands of Zerubbabel have laid the foundation of this temple; his hands will also complete it. Then you will know that the LORD Almighty has sent me to you."

Zechariah presents simple, yet intriguing imagery. Clearly there is a conflict underway in this passage. A "mighty mountain" is going to be destroyed by the efforts of a man with an odd-sounding name, Zerubbabel. Following the leveling of this great mountain, a stone will be brought out to the shouts of celebration. By implication, this stone, a "capstone," will complete a building of some kind, and in doing so demonstrate victory. And this character, Zerubbabel, will be responsible for the laying of the foundation of a temple as well as the completion of the overall structure.

In looking closer at this passage, numerous questions arise. What is being referred to as a "mighty mountain?" Who exactly is Zerubbabel, and what is he up to? What type of stone is this mysterious capstone and how is it a sign of completion and victory? Who is shouting in this victory celebration? And how does all this relate to a temple, whose foundation is laid, but is still awaiting completion?

The revelation behind these few simple verses provides the key to unlock *volumes* of Biblical prophecy regarding the first and the second coming of Jesus Christ. As soon as the reader of Zechariah gains a proper understanding of the scene in this core passage, and unlocks the meaning behind the mysterious capstone, a framework can be established that will shed light on many of the end-time, Biblical events.

That is, this passage from Zechariah is actually the hub of a much larger prophetic wheel, with all the other prophetic books in the Bible pointing back to the prophet's core thesis above. The lines that lead from this "hub" act like pointers on a grand map. Therefore, all other prophetic messages must fall into line with Zechariah's vision, including those images and events in the most famous prophetic book of all, the Book of Revelation.

Ironically, the Book of Zechariah has never fully received due recognition. This book has been considered a work by a minor prophet, and a parenthetical aside to the corpus of prophetic work in the Old Testament. The time has come, however, to let the prophet speak again, and for us to listen intently.

2

The Towers of Babel

In order to understand Zechariah's vision, and to unlock the meaning encased in his mysterious capstone, we must first turn to the early days of man on earth. This was a time when men were forming a new, unified civilization following the devastation of the Flood. The population of the earth came together under one rule and turned its combined focus towards a massive construction project - a tower - as their unifying purpose. This is the story of the Tower of Babel, and it brings to mind an image of worldwide, organized rebellion by mankind. The account, found in Genesis 11, is presented on the following page.

Such a simple story provides a look at the complex nature of man and the state of his heart. It also, surprisingly, points the way prophetically to the state of the world in the last days. The key points of this account are:

☐ The focal point of man's unification was a building project. The Hebrew word **migdal** translates into a number of images, but has always been understood to mean a "tower" because of its height.

☐ Man was of one "language" and one "speech." The Hebrew word for speech is alternatively used as *purpose* or *cause*. Therefore, this unified world power had a **single language** and a **single cause**.

Gen 11:1-9

Now the whole world had one language and a common speech. As men moved eastward, they found a plain in Shinar and settled there.

They said to each other, "Come, let's make bricks and bake them thoroughly." They used brick instead of stone, and tar for mortar. Then they said, "Come, let us build ourselves a city, with a tower that reaches to the heavens, so that we may make a name for ourselves and not be scattered over the face of the whole earth."

But the LORD came down to see the city and the tower that the men were building. The LORD said, "If as one people speaking the same language they have begun to do this, then nothing they plan to do will be impossible for them. Come, let us go down and confuse their language so they will not understand each other."

So the LORD scattered them from there over all the earth, and they stopped building the city. That is why it was called Babel--because there the LORD confused the language of the whole world. From there the LORD scattered them over the face of the whole earth.

☐ More specifically, man's "cause" at Babel had three related aspects: to make a name for himself, to not be scattered across the earth, and to reach the heavens. Underlying all three was the more sinister, core objective, shared by rebellious man throughout time. And this was to establish a throne on earth to rival the throne of God in heaven. The story of Babel can thus be summarized as: **man enthroning man as God**.

☐ Man was unsuccessful in his work because God intervened. The project ended prematurely, and the building became the ruins of the first, post-flood world order.

☐ As a result of God's intervention, mankind was divided into a multitude of differing languages and scattered by groups according to common language. These various linguistic groups then became nations, in essence, groups of men with differing purposes and agendas. Man became like dust and was scattered across the face of the whole earth.

The consequences of Babel were *confusion of speech* and the *disunity of purpose*. And this has been the case for the ensuing millennia. For thousands of years the peoples of earth have not been united in either language or purpose, and this is evidenced today by incidents of conflict and war. Other visible proofs around us include national borders, differing currency and measures, and various languages or tongues.

It is surprising, then, to find prophecies regarding a unified kingdom of man, a one-world government in the last days. Is it more than a coincidence that there is to come a global union of peoples that will erase national boundaries, remove differing currency and measures, and unite the world under one government? Will this end-time kingdom be formed in rebellion against God and therefore actually represent a second Tower of Babel? And will the single purpose of the leaders of this kingdom be enthroning a man as God?

2 Thess 2:3
...for that day will not come until **the rebellion occurs** and the **man of lawlessness** is revealed...

Paul confirms for us here that this day will not occur until a *second* great rebellion occurs, the first great rebellion having occurred at the Tower of Babel. In fact, the entire prophetic story of the coming end-time government of man could be described as "the second Babel" as it will be a global kingdom, formed in rebellion, which will unite man in both purpose and speech.

One book in particular sets the tone for the rest of the literature on the rebellion of the last days and the Messiah's return: the work of the prophet Zechariah.

Introduction to Zechariah

Zechariah tells so much of the story of the Messiah that he deserves a brief introduction. Simply stated, Zechariah packs a punch. In fourteen short chapters, the prophet makes more references to the first and second coming of the Messiah than any other book in the Old Testament, with the exception of Isaiah who took sixty-six chapters to do so![1] All of these prophecies, written over *five hundred years* before the Messiah's birth, came to pass and are still coming to pass through one person, Jesus Christ.

The prophet Zechariah held a unique place in the history of Israel. He was a prophet whose role was to lift the spirits of the Jews returning from exile, and to encourage them to rebuild the temple in Jerusalem following its destruction by the Babylonians. At various stages of the building process, the Israelites became frightened of their neighbors, or were distracted and lost interest, and their temple-building efforts stagnated. Zechariah tells them to let their "hands be strong" and to be diligent.

Zech 8:13
"As you have been an object of cursing among the nations, O Judah and Israel, so will I save you, and you will be a blessing. Do not be afraid, **but let your hands be strong.**"

The prophetic revelations in the book of Zechariah sew two events together with a single thread, these two events being the *first* and *second coming* of the Messiah. The two are presented side-by-side, or one on top of the other. It is as if the second coming is so thoroughly related to the first that they are both part of a single action! And in describing these two most important events in the divine plan for the world, he also foretells of a *second* Tower of Babel.

The Second Tower of Babel

As mentioned, Zechariah presents an incredible overview of the completed history of mankind.

ZECHARIAH 4

6   So he said to me, "This is the word of the LORD to Zerubbabel: 'Not by might nor by power, but by my Spirit,' says the LORD Almighty.

7   "What are you, O mighty mountain? Before Zerubbabel you will become level ground. Then he will bring out the capstone to shouts of 'God bless it! God bless it!'"

8   Then the word of the LORD came to me:

9   "The hands of Zerubbabel have laid the foundation of this temple; his hands will also complete it. Then you will know that the LORD Almighty has sent me to you."

The key to unlock the meaning of this passage, and to witness its incredible relevance for the rest of Scripture, is to understand the magnitude of what is being described. We know from other key, prophetic sources in the Bible that man is going to embark on a worldwide empire in the end times. The language the prophet uses here suggests that he is adding to our understanding of these end-time events.

We noted before that the end-time kingdom of man will be a reflection of the efforts of man at the original Tower of Babel, as told in Genesis. Now, in Zechariah, we have a single image that appears to describe the entire rebellious kingdom of the last days. All that is confronting the purposes of God's will on earth is described as a "mighty mountain." This mountain of opposition must be removed, this towering obstacle must be "leveled," before the full and complete victory of God is obtained over all creation.

Could it be that Zechariah has chosen the image of a mighty mountain to represent the unified rebellion of man in the last days because the original tower was just that, a mighty mountain? Is he drawing a parallel, visually, between the magnitude of man's rebellion in the last days and the size, and shape, of man's Tower at Babel following the flood?

Indeed, it appears so. The picture that Zechariah presents is the *ultimate defeat of the kingdom of Satan* followed by the *ultimate victory of the kingdom of God*, at the end of the age. The "mighty mountain" is Zechariah's way of presenting a parallel between the efforts of man in the earliest days of rebellion and the efforts of man in the worldwide rebellion of the last days.

The name that this future kingdom takes, we are told by numerous Biblical prophets, is "Babylon." This is hinted at by Jeremiah, Isaiah, John, and others. Originally, Babylon was the birthplace of the occult and the mystery religions following the flood, and an earthly center for the rebellion of the nations against God.[2] It was in the territory of Babylonia that the original Tower of Babel was built. Both facets, the occult and rebellion, manifested themselves on the Plain of Shinar as the first Tower was being raised, and both facets will manifest again in the coming global kingdom of man.

In fact the same word in Hebrew used for Babel is also used for Babylon; *they are one and the same*. Both words are represented by the following three Hebrew characters, read from right to left:

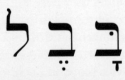

(*Babel* and *Babylon*)

Following the trail of Babel or Babylon (or בָּבֶל) throughout the Bible allows one to follow the spirit of rebellious man, and his attempts to create a throne for one of his own as God of the earth.

God's intervention marked the end of the physical Tower of Babel, but not its goal in the hearts of men. The end of the first tower was soon followed by the beginning of a second tower, this time a *figurative* or *spiritual* Tower of Babel. Work on this second Tower began as soon as an elite corps of men from various nations on earth attempted to reunite in language and purpose after they had been scattered across the face of the earth. And their attempts at unification continue today, in direct rebellion to God's plan for the destiny of mankind.

The two towers are summarized below:

Tower of Babel #1 - The original **physical Tower**, representing *man enthroning man as God,* on the Plain of Shinar at the beginning of civilization after the flood

Tower of Babel #2 - The figurative or **spiritual Tower**, a "mighty mountain," representing *man enthroning man as God* on a worldwide, geographical basis, reaching completion at the end of the age

Work on this second, figurative tower continued through the Babylonian Empire and its successors, the Medes and the Persians, the Greeks, the Romans, and even into the empires of Europe, including the Holy Roman Empire. Construction of this spiritual tower of Babel will end in the last days, when man is unified under a one-world political, economic, and religious system.

And it is with this image of the spiritual Tower of Babel that we return to Zechariah and the "mighty mountain." There is a confirmation of the link between the mountain found in Zechariah and the second, spiritual Tower of Babel; this is found in the words of the prophet Jeremiah.

Jer 51:24-25

"Before your eyes I will repay Babylon (**Babel -** בָּבֶל) and all who live in Babylonia for all the wrong they have done in Zion," declares the LORD. "I am against you, **O destroying mountain**, you who **destroy the whole earth**," declares the LORD.

The Babel (בָּבֶל) of prophecy is described as a "destroying mountain" in Jeremiah in the same sense that Zechariah describes it as a "mighty mountain." And this mountain is not limited to one geographical location, for it has the power to "destroy the whole earth." It is, in essence, the spiritual kingdom of Satan, the opposing kingdom to what Jesus came to establish two thousand years ago. It is against this mountain that the saints of the kingdom of God are currently contending in the spiritual realm, and the mountain therefore represents the source of all spiritual warfare and evil on earth. Zechariah is presenting two kingdoms in mortal conflict.

A further confirmation of this is found in the rather strange but hugely important name of "Zerubbabel." And in this name we see the signs of yet a third Tower of Babel.

A Third Tower of Babel?

The governor of the post-exilic Israelites was a historical figure named Zerubbabel, and he was responsible for organizing the returning mass of Israelites from their exile in the land of Babylonia. He was, by virtue of his position, the person responsible for the re-laying of the foundation of Solomon's Temple, at or around 536 BC. This relaying of the foundation was necessary because the temple was so severely destroyed by the invading forces of Babylon (or Babel) that it had to be rebuilt, from the ground up.

We learn of Zerubbabel and his rank in Haggai:

Hag 1:1-2

...the LORD came through the prophet Haggai to **Zerubbabel** son of Shealtiel, governor of Judah, and to Joshua son of Jehozadak, the high priest...

Zerubbabel, you might recall, is also mentioned in the core passage from Zechariah in connection to the "mighty mountain." He takes on a more mysterious nature when we learn that he is the one who will be responsible for the incredible defeat of the mighty mountain, the kingdom of Babel, in the last days.

Z4:7   "What are you, O mighty mountain? **Before Zerubbabel you will become level ground**."

And so Zerubbabel the governor is not the only one who is being referred to in the fourth chapter of Zechariah. There is someone of a much greater prophetic nature being referenced amidst the rubble of post-exilic Jerusalem. The key to unlock the meaning of this mysterious figure is in his name: Zerubbabel is really **Zerub – Babel**.

Zerub comes from the root word **zarab**, and means to "burn," to "scorch,"[3] and to "flow away." The second part of his name, **Babel**, is a reference to the Tower of Babel, where the division of man and the confusion of languages began (the Tower is literally written in his name: Babel – בָּבֶל). Zerubbabel, then, is a prophetic character who is going to be the source by which the confusion of languages and the disunity of man are to be burned up, destroyed forever, *reversed*. This is the man who is going to bring deliverance from the strife in the world, and who will remove the dissension that has raged in man's blood for thousands of years.

Beyond a shadow of doubt, the mysterious and prophetic figure of Zerubbabel is in fact the Messiah, **Jesus Christ.** And the "mighty mountain" represents all that stands in this great Deliverer's way. Jesus Christ is creating His own Tower, a single people and a holy nation, a people united through His righteousness.

Rev 5:9-10
"With your blood you **purchased men for God from every tribe** and **language** and **people** and **nation**. You have made them to be **a kingdom**..."

This collection of peoples is the ultimate accomplishment of what man attempted at the original Tower of Babel, and failed to bring into being. This single nation is being created by the true Messiah, and therefore this global project represents a *righteous* tower, the Tower of (Zerub)Babel.

Furthermore, the Tower of Zerub-Babel is the same as the "temple" under construction by the Messiah.

> **Z4:9** "The hands of Zerubbabel·have laid the foundation of this **temple**; his hands will also complete it.

Jesus' global kingdom is metaphorically referred to as a temple by Zechariah, and is a worldwide house of God. Just as Zerubbabel focused his efforts on the building of a temple in Jerusalem following the Babylonian exile, so now Jesus as Zerub-Babel focuses His efforts on the building of a far greater, spiritual temple that will unify the whole world. And work on this temple began on the cross in 33 A.D.

As a means of distinguishing between the historical and the prophetic Zerubbabels, the greater of the two will be referred to as "Zerub-Babel," designating the Messiah, Jesus Christ.

A Temple-Builder by Blood

The Messiah, however, is more than just a figurative temple builder; it is in his genes. Through His mother, Mary, and her bloodline, Jesus is descended from Zerubbabel (Luke 3:27), the man responsible for the construction of the temple in Jerusalem! The same lineage is true of his earthly father's family, through His adoption into Joseph's bloodline (Matt. 1:12). It is a startling fulfillment to Zechariah's prophecy to find that Jesus literally is Zerub-Babel both by bloodline and by His own efforts at building a new, spiritual temple on earth.

Zechariah later provides confirmation of Zerub-Babel's true character, and as to who therefore is building this new temple. As we know from Biblical prophecy, the Messiah was going to be a "branch" of the Lord, that was to grow out of the House of David.

Zech 6:11-13
"Tell him this is what the LORD Almighty says:
'Here is the man whose name is **the Branch**, and
he will branch out from his place and build the
temple of the LORD. **It is he who will build the
temple of the LORD**, and he will be clothed with
majesty and will sit and **rule on his throne.**'"

Here Zechariah answers the question subtly put forth in
his fourth chapter, as to who is Zerubbabel? And what is he
up to? It is Jesus Christ, and following the construction of
His temple, He is coming back to rule on His throne.

His name, Zerub-**Babel**, and his efforts suggest to us that
His temple will be a righteous Tower of Babel. It will be a
worldwide kingdom that will unify man in both purpose
and speech. Through the completion of this temple, Jesus
will have accomplished two key objectives: 1.) the destruction
of the counterfeit kingdom of Satan on earth (the "mighty
mountain"), and 2.) the unification of man into a single, holy
nation, reversing the effects of the original Tower.

1 Peter 2:9
But you are a **chosen people**, a royal priesthood, a
holy nation, a people belonging to God...

As an example of the first great accomplishment of Zerub-
Babel, to destroy the mountain, or kingdom of Satan, we learn
from John why the Messiah came two thousand years ago.
It was to destroy the evil that so widely plagues the earth. It
was the first step in destroying the mighty mountain.

1 John 3:8
The reason the Son of God appeared was to
destroy the devil's work.

The second great accomplishment of Zerub-Babel is the
creation of a single nation comprised of people from all
nations and all languages. We catch a glimpse of this work
in the Book of Daniel, in a night vision. Daniel sees an image
of Jesus, perhaps as Zerub-Babel, ruling over people from
all nations and all languages, people who are united in a
singular purpose. And that purpose is to worship the King.

Dan 7:13-14

"In my vision at night I looked, and there before
me was one like a son of man, coming with the
clouds of heaven…He was given authority, glory
and sovereign power; **all peoples, nations and
men of every language worshiped him.**"

The implication is that while the opposing kingdom – or
tower – will be destroyed, described as a mighty mountain,
Jesus' kingdom – or tower – will be everlasting; His kingdom
will never be destroyed. He will not scatter men like dust,
but will instead gather them in unity from the four corners
of the earth.

Luke 13:29-30

"People will come from **east** and **west** and **north**
and **south**, and will take their places at the feast
in the kingdom of God."

In this work, Zerub-Babel has purchased the "living
stones" He needs to build this new, global temple. These
stones are the believers who chose to follow Christ, and who
are being united into one kingdom.

1 Peter 2:4-5

As you come to him, the living Stone – rejected by
men but chosen by God and precious to him – you
also, like **living stones**, are being **built into a spiritual
house**

They are a people previously of many languages now
speaking in one voice, and a people previously with
conflicting interests now with a single purpose.

What building did the Messiah begin constructing at His
first coming that has not fully been completed as of today?
What temple, or tower, did Jesus Christ lay the foundation
for during His earthly ministry that will only be completed
when He returns again? The temple under construction by
Zerub-Babel is none other than **His Church**, the spiritual
house and dwelling of God's Spirit on earth. And this temple
is the third, yet righteous and victorious, Tower of Babel.

3

COMPARISONS

The tools are now available for us to capture the entire scene from Zechariah's core passage.

First, the scene opens with a major conflict underway. The satanic kingdom is under attack, and is represented in the form of a "mighty mountain." This mountain is going to be leveled by the hand of a man named Zerub-*Babel*, and his name cleverly draws our attention to the original Tower of Babel. The symbol of a mighty mountain is in fact chosen as a means of drawing a parallel to the original Tower of Babel, which was apparently also a "mighty mountain." The mountain in Zechariah therefore represents a *figurative* Tower of Babel, a worldwide system of government that will unify man in purpose and speech during the end times. Both the original and the figurative Towers unite mankind in rebellion against God. Because of this, the second Tower, like the first, will be destroyed, through "the power and might of the Holy Spirit."

Zerub-Babel is not in fact the historic governor of the returning exiles, but rather a prophetic image of Jesus Christ, the Branch. And upon the destruction of the "mighty mountain" of Babel in the last days, a freshly completed temple will be established. This new temple, like the opposing mighty mountain before it, is a worldwide kingdom or tower, yet a body of believers known as the Church, the holy nation of the saints of God.

One kingdom will fall, and another will rise!

According to Zechariah, the foundation for this new temple (or kingdom) was to be laid by Jesus Christ, and He will also be responsible for its completion.

> **Z4:9** "The hands of Zerubbabel have **laid the foundation** of this temple; his hands will also **complete it.**"

The completion will be evidenced by the appearance of a *mysterious capstone*.

> **Z4:7** "**Then he will bring out the** *capstone* to shouts of 'God bless it! God bless it!'"

Zerubbabel's relevance to the underlying mystery is clearer once his name has been divided with a hyphen, as in **Zerub-Babel**. With this, we see that Zechariah has revealed to us the "One who will separate us from the kingdom of darkness" (Babel). At the same time, we have learned that this Zerub-Babel is the "One who will build His own Temple;" that is, the kingdom of God on earth. And, lastly, we learn that Zerub-Babel is the "One who will remove the curse" of the first Tower of Babel, forever.

What exactly is the curse that remains on man since the first Tower? The *physical effects* of this curse include the scattering of mankind through disunity and the confusion of languages. The *spiritual effects* of Babel include the manipulation of the nations by the demonic powers and principalities against which we wage war (Eph. 6:12). All of these consequences are the curses laid on the back of unrepentant, rebellious, and prideful man.

Jesus, in His role as Zerub-Babel, calls His people out of Babel, reunites them into one nation and one language, and removes these curses from their midst. This work, which began at the cross, continues today through the power and might of the Holy Spirit, and will be completed at the fall of the figurative Tower of Babel, at the end of the age.

Three Babels Compared

The contrast between the two unrighteous Towers of Babel and the righteous Tower of Zerub-Babel can now be seen in greater detail. There is much to glean from the comparison of the three and it is worth analyzing the nature of these differences. The source of our comparison lies, as before, in the center of Zechariah's core passage.

These few verses from Zechariah lay out like a comparative list: on the left side we have the Righteous Tower, on the right side we have *both* of the unrighteous Towers, the physical Tower that was destroyed in Genesis and the spiritual Tower which will be destroyed in the future. The second, spiritual version is representative of Satan's kingdom on earth today, a kingdom that will reach its zenith through the formation of a one-world government in rebellion to God.

The Towers Contrasted

The Righteous Tower	The Unrighteous Towers
Jesus is the Architect	Satan is the Architect
Jesus is Establishing a Temple and a Throne on Earth	Satan is Establishing a Temple and a Throne on Earth
The Temple will be built by the might and the power of the Holy Spirit, working through redeemed man	The Temple will be built through the might and power of rebellious man empowered by evil spirits
The Temple will be completed	The Temple will be leveled
The sign of the Temple being completed will be the appearance of a stone, a "capstone"	The sign of the Temple nearing completion will also be the appearance of a stone
The Temple will successfully unite man in language and in purpose	The Temple will come close to uniting man in language and in purpose, but will fail in the end

1. Who Is Doing The Building?

Jesus, as Zerub-Babel, is the one who came to establish a new, righteous Tower. This Tower is a new Temple or House of God on earth, the place of His dwelling. It is a building with no geographical limits that is filled with the presence of His Holy Spirit. Jesus is the author of our faith, and the Holy Spirit is the overseer of the construction project on the ground, until the Messiah's return.

On the other hand, Satan is also building a Tower. His Tower is also a global, spiritual Temple, a house of a false god. The archenemy of God was responsible for the behind-the-scenes orchestration of the first Tower, and he will do the same for the spiritual Tower at the end of the age.

2. What Is The Purpose of the Tower?

The focal point of the Lord's work is the building of a global kingdom, symbolically presented as a "temple." The Church is in fact His kingdom and tower on earth. Through this kingdom He will restore the fullness of the fellowship that the Creator once had with man in the Garden of Eden. Furthermore, He will shape and mold the saints of His kingdom into the governing authorities of His Millennial Rule, thus fulfilling man's original destiny to become children and heirs of God. And from this spiritual building the Messiah will establish His Throne for an earthly rule.

Rev 20:6
...they will be priests of God and of Christ and will **reign with him for a thousand years**.

The focal point of Satan's work is establishing his own global kingdom and tower, through rebellion to God. This building project is referred to as a mighty, destroying mountain. He, too, is working to shape and mold man into his image and according to his designs. His temple will serve as the throne of his doomed earthly rule, the seat of power for the worldwide kingdom that is destroyed in the last days.

3. How Will These Temples Be Built?

The true Church will be built *solely* by the Spirit of God, the Holy Spirit. As such, it is not a physical building, but rather a spiritual building. No man will be able to boast in the kingdom of God. It was not by man's might or power that the foundation stone for this temple was laid at Jesus' death on the cross, and it will not be by man's might or power that the temple will be completed.

Z4:6 "Not by might nor by power, **but by my Spirit,**" says the LORD Almighty.

To paraphrase, "Not by human might, nor by human power shall the kingdom of God be established on earth, but only by the power and the might of the Holy Spirit!"

By contrast, the first Tower was, and the second spiritual Tower will be, the product of man's might and power in conjunction with the occult powers of rebellion and witchcraft.

1 Sam 15:23
"For **rebellion** is as the sin of **witchcraft**..."

Witchcraft is essentially the manipulation and control of man through spiritual forces. Hence, rebellious man was encouraged by the manipulation and control of demonic forces at the first Tower. In contrast to the power and might of the Holy Spirit, there was human might and human power in unison with evil spirits. The same will be true of the kingdom of Babel to come.

4. Which Construction Project Will Have Success?

The righteous Tower of Zerub-Babel will be finished, whereas the original Tower of Babel was left unfinished. For what man could not achieve on his own, through rebellion and pride, the Lord will accomplish through the power of His Spirit.

Z4:9 "The hands of Zerubbabel have laid the foundation of this temple; **his hands will also complete it.**"

As the first Tower failed to accomplish its goal, so too will the end-time spiritual Tower of Babel not reach its full potential. God always intervenes on man's behalf, and the Lord will return to rescue His people and destroy the evil empire of Satan. Even if at the last moment, in the darkest hour, the Messiah will descend to the earth with a mighty battle cry, like a "pent-up flood." And spiritual Babel will be brought to its knees, destroyed forever.

Z4:7   "What are you, O mighty mountain? **Before Zerubbabel you will become level ground.**"

5. What Will Be The Sign Of Completion?
The sign of completion of Jesus' temple, the third and righteous Tower of Babel, will be the presentation of a single stone, the mysterious *capstone*. From Zechariah we get the sense that the capstone is somehow related to Jesus as the returning and triumphant Messiah.

Z4:7   *"Then* **he will bring out the capstone** to shouts of 'God bless it! God bless it!'"

Upon the presentation of the capstone at the end of the age, the Lord will have completed His work. The temple building project that began at the cross will finally have reached its completion. And the world will enter into rest from its temple-building efforts.

Satan's temple, on the other hand, will also be built. The evidence of this is the mighty mountain before Zerub-Babel. However, this building project will not reach its completion and will prove unsuccessful, primarily due to the presence of the Church and the nation of Israel. These two, interrelated groups of people will represent the incomplete nature of Satan's global rule, and the lack of a true worldwide unity of purpose. And this will be the underlying source of great persecution.

6. What Will Be The Result Of This Project?

As a result of the work of Jesus as Zerub-Babel, men of all nations and tongues will be united under one King, and they will have a new language and a single purpose. It will be the ultimate fulfillment of the *Righteous* Tower of Babel: a universal kingdom of God on earth.

Isa 9:6-7

For to us a child is born, to us a son is given, and the government will be on his shoulders. And he will be called Wonderful Counselor, Mighty God, Everlasting Father, Prince of Peace. **Of the increase of his government and peace there will be no end.**

The comparison of the Towers is powerful, and leads to a number of revelations. One is a realization that redeemed man will have a new tongue, a **single language**. A new language is one of the two strategic accomplishments of Zerub-Babel as Jesus Christ. That is, the objective of Zerub-Babel is to fully reverse the effect, or curse, of the Tower of Babel, and so a new purpose for man and a new language for man are inextricably *tied together*. This work of the Messiah will result in the creation of a new voice for His spiritual temple, the Church.

This new voice first occurred at Pentecost, when the followers of Jesus spoke in a new language or "tongue." This was the specific sign, chosen by God, to demonstrate the creation of a new kingdom, a kingdom created by the power and the might of His Holy Spirit. And this new voice continues to operate today, as referred to by the Apostles and at various points in the Book of Acts. Paul, for instance, states about his personal prayer language:

1 Cor 14:18-19
I thank God that I speak in tongues more than
all of you.

The Lord intends for His people to be united through
the workings of the spiritual gifts described in First
Corinthians, on a personal and on a corporate level. And the
primary gift is the gift of a new language. The Church is to
function as one body, and speak one language, as a sign of
harmony in the Body of Christ. There must, therefore, be great
power in this unifying spoken word!

This realization helps solve a mystery in Paul's writings.
It is why "tongues" are referred to as a "sign for unbelievers."
This new language is a sign of the success of **Zerub-Babel** in
destroying the curse of the original Tower at Babel, and in
accomplishing what man tried to do through rebellion but
failed: unity on earth in purpose and speech. Paul is telling
the world to take notice of this accomplishment!

1 Cor 14:22
Tongues, then, are a sign, not for believers **but
for unbelievers**...

4

THE TEMPLES OF GOD

Jesus Christ, as Zerub-Babel, is the builder of a new house of God. Work on this building began when He died on the cross for our sins, and then rose from the dead three days later. We find evidence of this in John's gospel.

John 2:19-21
Jesus answered them, "Destroy this temple, and I will raise it again in three days." The Jews replied, "It has taken forty-six years to build this temple, and you are going to raise it in three days?" **But the temple he had spoken of was his body.**

What man cannot accomplish, because of the disunity and conflict from Babel, God has already accomplished through the precious life of His only Son. Through this doorway all men have the ability to enter into a single, holy nation under the headship and authority of Jesus Christ.

This new nation is comprised of people from all nations, races and languages. All of these lives represent the followers of Jesus; they are the body of believers, His Church. They also represent stones in this new temple of God.

1 Peter 2:4-5
As you come to him, the living Stone...you also, like **living stones**, are being **built into a spiritual house**...

In line with the temples of the Old Covenant, this new, greater temple assumes all of the previous titles for the dwelling place of God. It is the *house* of God, which is the same as the place of God's *dwelling*, and this is the same as the *tabernacle*. This equation of terms is brought out in a concise way in Psalm 27:

> **Ps 27:4-5**
> One thing I ask of the LORD, this is what I seek: that I may dwell in the **house of the LORD** all the days of my life, to gaze upon the beauty of the LORD and to seek him **in his** *temple*. For in the day of trouble he will keep me safe **in his** *dwelling*; he will hide me in the **shelter of his** *tabernacle*...

To understand this new temple, it is helpful to first understand the meaning behind the previous temples. These were the physical temples of God, referred to as the *tabernacle* and *temple* in the Old Testament.

The Old Covenant

A cursory walk through the Old Testament will reveal a number of temples (or tabernacles) that served as the House of the Lord. Each temple was a place of worship, and was a "house" for God where He dwelt with His people. As such, each temple represented a place where God could commune directly with men, as He first did in the Garden, and where men could give thanks in return for His faithfulness, mercy and compassion. The people of Israel were represented at these meetings by the official priesthood, and they gave thanks to God through offerings of tithes, incense, animals and worship.

There is, however, another purpose for God's temple that is often overlooked. And it is this often ignored and least understood purpose that plays a crucial role in the mystery before us. Temples were built to house the **throne of God**, and they held the seat of His power and authority on earth. More specifically, the innermost room of the temple served as the *throne room*, and it was in this chamber that the earthly court of the King was in session.

The inner room of the temple housed the throne. This was a veiled chamber in the Tabernacle that later became the innermost room of Solomon's Temple. It was referred to as the "Holiest of Holies" and was where the Ark of the Covenant was kept. Resting on top of the Ark was a cover known as the Mercy Seat, and this royal seat was surrounded by two angels called "Cherubim" that were made out of hammered gold. **The Mercy Seat on the Ark was the throne; it was God's one and only throne on earth!** And it was placed in His throne room, the Holiest of Holies, where His presence manifested to commune with, and provide counsel to, His people.

2 Sam 6:2
...the ark of God, which is called by the Name, the name of the LORD Almighty, who is *enthroned* **between the cherubim that are on the ark.**

Ps 99:1-2
The LORD reigns, let the nations tremble; he **sits** *enthroned* **between the cherubim** [*on the Mercy Seat*], let the earth shake. Great is the LORD in Zion; he is exalted over all the nations.

The location of God's throne, and the temple that housed it, changed over time. A brief summary of these Old Testament temples is provided below:

1. **The Tabernacle of Moses**
    This is the first temple, and was carried across the wilderness for forty years, until it was eventually established in Canaan on Mount Gibeon. This temple was a tabernacle, or a large tent. The God of all creation chose to place His throne on earth in the humblest of surroundings. Compare this to the elaborate shrines built to false gods throughout the world!

2. **The Tabernacle of David**

Four hundred years after the creation of the first Tabernacle, King David was led to move the Ark out of the tent of Moses and into a new home, on Mount Zion. This was a new Tabernacle. David, however, was forbidden from building a permanent temple for God out of stone because he had shed blood. In a verse referencing his son, Solomon, and in a greater sense his future descendant, Jesus as Zerub-Babel, King David is told by Nathan the prophet that his offspring will build not just a temple but an *eternal kingdom*.

2 Sam 7:12-13

"When your days are over and you rest with your fathers, I will raise up your **offspring** to succeed you, who will come from your own body, and **I will establish his kingdom**. He is the one who will build a house for my Name, and **I will establish the throne of his kingdom forever**."

3. **The Temple of Solomon**

This is perhaps the most famous of all Temples, because of its reputation for glory and splendor. It was a magnificent, rectangular building with an outer court, an inner room for the priests and the veiled Holiest of Holies. The focus of the world today has returned to the Temple of Solomon because the rebuilding of this temple is a goal of the modern Jewish nation. Biblical prophecy implies that Israel will attempt to rebuild the Temple of Solomon on its original site, on the Temple Mount.

The first three temples were houses of ordinance and law. God's chosen people were given the opportunity to demonstrate righteousness by adhering to specific rules and regulations. The lesson God was teaching all of mankind through the Israelites was simple and effective: righteousness through works and the law is *unattainable*.

The New Covenant
Foundation Stone

Jesus replaced the first covenant with a better covenant, and created a more powerful relationship between man and God. In the same sense, God replaced the physical Temple of Solomon with a greater Temple of Zerub-Babel. This occurred at the cross. This new covenant is based on grace through faith in the redemptive, shed blood of His Son, Jesus Christ. God so loved the world that he sent His only Son, to die for it.

Jesus coming to earth the first time was likened to a stone from heaven being laid at the foundation of a temple on earth. The prophet Isaiah informs us of this: a stone was going to be laid in Zion...

Isa 28:16
"See, I lay a **stone** in Zion"

This is a reference to Jesus as the foundation stone for the new house of God, Zerub-Babel's global temple. The Hebrew word for "lay" is **yoceed**, or **yacad**, and is translated "to set, to found, to settle." The death of Jesus on the cross signifies the foundation stone, and His brief entombment represents the foundation-laying ceremony for this new building.

The symbolism of the laying of a foundation stone is actually part of an ancient tradition that dates back to the earliest civilizations of man. In times past, the foundation of a building was represented by a single stone, and this stone was covered with the blood of a sacrifice of some kind. In Israel, the sacrifice of an animal on the freshly laid foundation stone was a means of dedicating the building to God, and was thought to contribute to the spiritual health of those who were to live inside. The future inhabitants were, in essence, dedicated to God through the covenant shedding of blood.

Furthermore, the *foundation stone* and the *doorway* into a building were related. We see elements of this tradition at the first Passover, when the Hebrews were enslaved in Egypt. God told the Hebrews through Moses to sprinkle the blood from a lamb on the doorway to their homes, and this act guaranteed the spiritual health of those inside, especially the first-born males. In his treatise on old-world threshold covenants, Trumbull expresses this relationship between thresholds (or door lintels) and foundation stones:

> "The foundation stone of a new building is...the threshold [*doorstep*] of that structure. Hence to lay the foundations in blood is to proffer blood at the threshold. Traces of this custom are to be found in the practices or the legends of peoples...all the world over. Apparently the earlier sacrifices were of human beings. Later they were of animals substituted for persons."[4]

And so Jesus' death on the cross represents both the *foundation stone* underneath the new temple, and the *doorway* into this new temple. As Jesus remarks:

Matt 7:8
"For everyone who asks receives; he who seeks finds; and **to him who knocks, the door will be opened**."

And to His saints, Jesus proclaims the assurance of their salvation:

Rev 3:8
"See, I have placed before you **an open door that no one can shut**."

Likewise, Jesus refers to Himself as the Way, and that no one can come to God unless they go (or walk) through Him, and over the precious blood on the threshold.

John 14:6
"I am **the way** and the truth and the life. No one comes to the Father **except through me**."

As mentioned, Jesus was descended from Zerubbabel, through Mary's bloodline, and therefore had temple-building blood in his veins. Through adoption into Joseph's family, Jesus was also descended from Solomon, the first temple builder. It is fitting then to find Jesus *removing the need for* the physical temples of Solomon and Zerubbabel, and the covenant which they represented. He began the construction of a new spiritual temple that extended beyond the borders of Israel. It was to be a *worldwide* house of God that allowed access for both Jew *and* Gentile. And since His ascension to heaven, it has been the work of the Holy Spirit to continue to build the Lord's temple, one living and redeemed stone at a time.

1 Peter 2:4-5

As you come to him, the living Stone-rejected by men but chosen by God and precious to him- **you also, like living stones, are being built into a spiritual house...**

The purpose of this temple is clear: salvation and eternal fellowship with God through entry into a new, *spiritual* Holiest of Holies. This new innermost room is a place of grace, mercy and compassion. It is a place of refuge and shelter.

Prior to this, only the chief priest had access to the throne room, during only one day of the year. At the moment of Jesus' death on the cross, the veil in the temple that separated the Holiest of Holies from the outside world was torn completely in half.

Matt 27:50-51

And when Jesus had cried out again in a loud voice, he gave up his spirit. At that moment the curtain of the temple was **torn in two** from top to bottom.

This torn veil symbolized the free access of future generations into the very throne room of God. Now we, as individuals, have access to the spiritual Holiest of Holies, the very throne of God in this new temple. And, we can approach the throne of God with boldness and confidence!

Heb 4:16
Let us then approach the **throne of grace with
confidence**, so that we may receive mercy and
find grace to help us in our time of need.

Our free access to the throne room of God is a
demonstration of the Messiah's love, a love that is so much
greater than anything we can imagine. His love is beyond
our human understanding; it surpasses our own experiences
and knowledge of love.

Eph 3:18-19
...to grasp how wide and long and high and deep
is **the love of Christ**, and to know **this love that
surpasses knowledge**...

The Fourth and Final House of God

Zechariah has told us, in his core passage, that Jesus
Christ as Zerub-Babel laid the first stone in a new temple,
and that He will lay the final stone in this temple as well. In
the meantime, the Holy Spirit continues the temple-building
efforts on earth, and completes the section in between. This
is a temple of God's unique design.

What God did on earth was often representative of a
pattern that existed in heaven. This is precisely what the
author of Hebrews informs us about the Tabernacle:

Heb 8:4-5
They [*the high priests*] serve at a sanctuary that is
a **copy and shadow of what is in heaven**.

The shape, however, of this new spiritual temple, the
fourth temple, has remained a mystery for two thousand
years. Some have suggested that it is like the first two temples
and thus a tent or tabernacle. Others have proposed that it is
like the third, a magnificent building with two rooms and
an outer court. And still, there are those who suggest it is
something related to all three and yet unique in its own way.

Perhaps if we look to heaven first, we will learn more
about this spiritual temple on earth.

5

THE HEAVENLY THRONE

Heaven is a fascinating subject. The pattern that exists above is demonstrated for us on earth, although in less perfect and inferior ways. Earthly government and kingship are one example. We have a King in heaven, and there are kings and various forms of leadership on earth. Likewise, there is a hierarchy in the heavenly kingdom and there is a hierarchy in earthly kingdoms. There is a temple in heaven, and there is a temple on earth. The underlying principle is that there is a spiritual counterpart to certain key things we see in the physical, and there exists physical demonstrations on earth of things in heaven.

Ancient man was well versed in this concept, known as "as above, so below." We catch a glimpse of this concept when Jesus speaks to Peter:

Matt 16:19
"...whatever you **bind on earth** will be **bound in heaven**, and whatever you **loose on earth** will be **loosed in heaven**."

We also see this truth reflected in the Lord's Prayer:

Matt 6:9-10
"...your will be done **on earth as it is in heaven**."

Throughout Scripture there is an overabundance of descriptive imagery that suggests that God's dwelling and throne in heaven is similar *in type*, but different *in magnitude*, from what it was on earth. These references include visions and prophecies of the prophets, and revelations of the apostles. One poignant example of this is found in Hebrews 12:20, which concerns God's city in heaven.

Heb 12:22
But you have come to **Mount Zion**, to **the heavenly Jerusalem**, the **city of the living God**.

The city of God in heaven, referred to as the "heavenly Jerusalem," is called **Mount Zion** by the author of Hebrews. This heavenly city is presumably where God's throne resides. However, we know that there is also a physical Mount Zion on earth, located in Jerusalem. And we are led to conclude that this earthly mount is a type or representation of its counterpart in heaven. The Psalms, for instance, refer numerous times to the physical mountain in Jerusalem.

Ps 74:2
Remember the people you purchased of old, the tribe of your inheritance, whom you redeemed— **Mount Zion, where you dwelt**.

The earthly Mount Zion was in fact the central mount in Jerusalem, and was also known as Mount Moriah, and the City of David. It was here on this mountain that Solomon's Temple was erected, and this elevated site is referred to as the "Temple Mount." It was where God's earthly throne was housed, in the Holiest of Holies, at the highest place or summit of this mount.

The passage from Hebrews implies that God resides on a mount or mountain in heaven (Mount Zion), in the same sense He resided on a mount or mountain on earth (Mount Zion). His throne, whether on earth or in heaven, resides on the top of a mountain called Zion.

Yet the earthly Mount Zion is nothing to brag about.

Jerusalem has an altitude of just over 2,400 feet.[5] Contrast this with the tallest mountain on earth, Mount Everest, which is over 29,000 feet! Clearly, earthly Mount Zion was not chosen by God because of its impressive height. Rather, earthly Mt. Zion was specifically chosen to be less than magnificent. The Lord was demonstrating a key principle in His kingdom, one that has always been difficult for man to understand. This principle says that the least will be the greatest, and the lowly or humble will be exalted.

On the Utmost Heights of the Sacred Mountain

There are fascinating passages in the Bible that reveal the shape and location of the throne of God in heaven.

The prophet Ezekiel, for instance, writes of the Lord chastising the devil for being the one who first rebelled. As a result, he was cast out of heaven. Prior to his rebellion, though, the devil was known as Lucifer and served among the highest ranking angels in heaven. He was in fact ordained as a "guardian cherub." Lucifer had access to the very throne, or mount, of God.

Ezek 28:14-16
You were anointed as a guardian cherub, for so I ordained you. You were on **the holy mount of God**; you walked among the fiery stones...I drove you in disgrace from the **mount of God**, and I expelled you, O guardian cherub, from among the fiery stones.

The devil is described as having walked on the *holy mount* of God. Isaiah confirms that the most sacred place in heaven is on the top of a mountain, where again the devil (Lucifer) is specifically accused of trying to steal the throne of God.

Isa 14:12-13
You said in your heart, "I will ascend to heaven; I will raise my throne above the stars of God; **I will sit enthroned on the mount of assembly, on the utmost heights of the sacred mountain.**"

Where did Satan want to sit? He wanted to be like God and sit enthroned in heaven on the *utmost heights* of the *sacred mountain*!

The conclusion we can draw from Hebrews, Ezekiel, and Isaiah is that God reigns from His throne in heaven, atop a mountain, just as He did in the Old Covenant when His earthly throne resided in the Holiest of Holies, atop a mountain. And as the author of Hebrews points out, both mountains are known as "Mount Zion."

This heavenly throne is also where Jesus reigns today. He has been there, at the right hand of God, ever since His death on the cross and subsequent resurrection to eternal life.

Luke 22:69
"But from now on, the Son of Man will be seated
at the **right hand of the mighty God.**"

And both the Son and the Father are enthroned in heaven in such a way that no one, in heaven or on earth, is able to exalt himself above their throne. Their throne represents the highest place in heaven, and indeed the universe.

Ps 97:9
For you, O LORD, are the Most High over all the earth; you are **exalted far above all gods**.

And so we have a picture of a heavenly mountain, both high and great, and on the summit of this mountain rests the throne of God and the resurrected Messiah. This paints a fascinating picture of heaven and God's throne. It is also a parallel to what we find on earth, where the throne of God, the Mercy Seat of the Ark, rested *at the summit* of the less impressive, physical Mount Zion.

Interestingly, the revelation that God lives on the top of a mountain, and rules from His throne on the summit, was of common knowledge to mankind ever since the beginning of civilization. Across the world, and through various languages and cultures, there has always been the notion that the supreme God is enthroned on a mountain on earth, and that this earthly mountain is a reflection of a sacred mountain and throne in heaven.

Mountain Temples

There are many examples of this theme among religions throughout time, across differing civilizations and languages. The throne of the gods was often referred to as the "world-mountain" and was the home for both a supreme being and his pantheon of lesser deities. Uno Holmberg, a recognized scholar of comparative religion, noted that:

> "The majority of the peoples of Central Asia have tales of a mighty world-mountain, which the Mongols and Kalmucks call Sumur or Sumer, and the Buriats Sumbur...The folk tales tell of a distant time, when Sumur was only a very little hill. Now its summit aspires to heights unattainable by man, offering thus to the gods a dwelling-place worthy of them."[6]

While this dwelling of the gods exists on earth, there was also a counterpart in heaven, just as we saw in the passage from the Book of Hebrews.

> "It is worthy of note that this mythical mountain is often placed in Heaven itself. Thus, the Over-god...lives in heaven on a 'golden mountain.' Similarly, the tales of the Yakutes tell of the 'milky-white stone mountain' of Heaven."[7]

In some cases, ancient man saw the summit as the throne, in other cases the summit was a temple or sanctuary, and still in others, the summit was a castle or fortress that housed both the temple and the throne.

The name "Sumer" in fact applied to one of the earliest civilizations on earth, located in what is today Iraq. This people worshiped at the temple of a *great mountain*. Their supreme god was known as Enlil, and his mountain and temple were referred to as E-kur ("kur" is the Sumerian word for mountain). This mountain served as the spiritual center for the kingdom of Sumer. According to a translation of *Enlil in the E-kur* we read:

> "In the city, the holy settlement of Enlil, in Nibru, the beloved shrine of father Great Mountain, he has made the dais of abundance, the E-kur, the shining temple, rise from the soil; he has made it grow on pure land as high as a towering mountain. Its prince, the Great Mountain, father Enlil, has taken his seat on the dais of the E-kur, the lofty shrine. No god can cause harm to the temple's divine powers. "[8]

The "dais" referred to above is a raised platform for the throne of the supreme god, located *at the summit* of the "Great Mountain."

The same was true of the ancient Persians, who referred to the world-mountain as Mount Alburz and whose peak was known as "Tera." According to their beliefs, at the summit there was a bridge, called "Chinvat," which led to the afterlife, and where the souls of men would travel either to heaven or to hell.[9] The peak, therefore, served as the throne of the supreme god, and from there he communed with man. As well, the summit served as a place of judgment.

Mount Olympus is perhaps the most well-known "world-mountain" in man's history. According to the mythology of the ancient Greeks, Zeus, the father of the gods, reigned from his lofty throne atop Mt. Olympus. Joining him on his sacred mountain were the chief gods of Greek mythology. As we see with the dual nature of Mount Zion in Hebrews, there was a heavenly Mt. Olympus and an earthly Mt. Olympus. The earthly version is situated on the tallest mountain in Greece, at 9570 feet.[10]

As well, the early tribesmen of Japan saw Mount Fiji as the sacred mountain of the supreme god Ainu. Today, Buddhists still refer to this mountain as a gateway to another world, and the Shintoists consider it the sacred home of their chief goddess.[11]

In the same way, the Aborigines pay homage to a giant limestone mound they refer to as Uluru, or what the

Australians refer to as Ayers Rock. The giant rock represents a convergence of many of their religious themes and myths.[12]

The Chinese have numerous sacred mountains, according to their pantheon of gods. And the Tibetan celestial city is Lhasa, and their spiritual leader, the Dalai Lama, resides in a palace with a golden roof on top of a mountain, Marpori.

Clearly there is a similarity among cultures with regard to their belief in a world-mountain and their knowledge of its heavenly counterpart. The question arises as to whether the earliest of God's chosen people, the early fathers of the Hebrew nation who lived prior to the tabernacle and prior to the construction of the Ark of the Covenant, demonstrated knowledge of this concept. This list includes men like Noah, Abraham, Isaac, and Jacob (Israel).

Interestingly, we find this particular belief underlying the construction of their ancient altars of sacrifice.

Ancient Altars

Since the time of Noah, God's chosen people have displayed a consistent knowledge of, and dedication to, the building of altars to the Lord. When the patriarchs had a significant spiritual experience, they erected a monument of stones, in some form, and dedicated the site as an altar to the Lord. They sacrificed animals on the top of the altar and then burned the meat. The list of those who performed this act of worship is quite long, and a few are presented below.

Following the flood, and the great boat coming to rest in the mountains of Ararat, Noah built an altar to the Lord on the dry ground.

Gen 8:20-21

Then Noah built an **altar** to the LORD and, taking some of all the clean animals and clean birds, he sacrificed burnt offerings on it.

The text tells us that Noah sacrificed burnt offerings on the top of the altar. In the same manner, Abraham built altars to the Lord on a number of occasions, and sacrificed to the

Lord, as detailed in Genesis 12.

And so the tradition continued. Jacob built a number of altars to the Lord, and one in particular is of interest. He built an altar as a memorial or sign of a covenant with his father-in-law Laban. And in this particular reference, we get a very specific glimpse of the shape of an altar. This monument is referred to as a "heap." The King James translation brings out some interesting details:

Gen 31:45-49

And Jacob said unto his brethren, Gather stones; and they took stones, and **made an heap**: and they did eat there **upon the heap**.... Jacob called it Galeed...and Mizpah... (KJV)

A heap of stones implies a mound-like appearance, and a mound is a smaller model of a mountain. Jacob and his father-in-law named the heap Galeed and Mizpah. The first name means a "heap of testimony." The second name actually means "watchtower" in Hebrew, suggesting something of considerable height with a level top. In addition, the King James translation says more specifically that Jacob and his relatives ate "upon" (or on top of) the heap. This suggests a rather large and level platform at the summit. They offered sacrifices "upon" the heap as well.

Moses later received instructions for the construction of altars under the requirements of the law. These altars were to be constructed in a specific way, according to a "building code" required by God. The *International Standard Bible Encyclopaedia* comments on these building instructions given by the Lord to Moses for the construction of altars. The altars were to have slopes instead of steps…

"Altars are commanded to be made of earth or of unhewn stone, yet so as to have, not steps, but only slopes for ascent to the same…implying that they stood on some elevation."[13]

The consensus among scholars is that these altars had sloped sides, with level platforms at the top, and that they stood *at considerable height*. Most Bible commentaries seem to agree: the altar was a "high heap" of stones that had a level top or platform for sacrifice. Small altars would appear as mounds, larger altars would appear as hills, and the largest would appear as mountains of stone.

For instance, according to *The New Unger's Bible Dictionary*, the earliest altars were a simple elevation of earth, rough stones, or turf. An altar that was to be used for sacrifice was a heap of stones with a "large, flat stone placed upon its top."[14] This seems to be in line with all of the passages above. The altar or "heap" built by Jacob is particularly revealing as evidence for this description.

And *Fausset's Bible Dictionary* refers to the Hebrew altar as "an elevation or high place: not the site, but the erections on them…"[15]

The manner of constructing an altar in the form of a heap of stones is therefore by God's design. The point implied through this is not that the altars of the patriarchs in the pre-Tabernacle era were built to look like the heavenly mountain of God; they were in fact "heaps." And the instructions given to Moses were clear: the altars were to be constructed of uncut stones, hardly resulting in a polished effect. The underlying point is, however, that in these heaps of stone or altars *lay an image* of the far more superior and perfect mountain of God in heaven, however subtle this reference may have been.

When the sacrifices were pleasing to God, His presence would descend upon the top of the altar. And for that brief moment in time, the elevated, level platform at the top became God's seat on earth, *His throne*, and the place of communion with His chosen people. The meaning is beautiful: the Lord leaves His heavenly dwelling to commune with His people on earth, and in both places the Lord is at home, on a mount, where He is exalted on His throne.

Key Truths Revealed

What can be learned from this stroll through scriptural references to temples, mountains, and altars?

First, God rules from His throne atop a heavenly mountain, a sacred mount, and Jesus is at His right hand. This is the heavenly Mount Zion.

Second, God chooses to replicate on earth what He has ordained in heaven. There is often a physical representation on earth for a spiritual truth in the heavenly realm. During the time of the Old Covenant, the heavenly throne of God was replicated on the earthly Mount Zion in Jerusalem.

Third, God's throne on earth was positioned atop the Mercy Seat on the Ark of the Covenant. And the Ark, like the throne in heaven, was placed on the highest point on the Mount Zion, the summit.

Fourth, prior to the creation of a tabernacle or temple, we see a reflection of the sacred mountain in heaven in the less than perfect and far inferior altars of the patriarchs. These were heaps of stones, with level tops, upon which sacrifices were placed.

Finally, Jesus came to destroy the earthly temple, and in doing so created an eternal, spiritual temple, known as His Church.

Before we can fully understand the mystery of the new, spiritual temple under construction by Zerub-Babel, we must first understand the unique role of the mysterious stone referred to as the "capstone." In doing so, we will resolve *five thousand years of mystery*.

PART II

THE MYSTERY RESOLVED

6

THE CAPSTONE REVEALED

The central point in the mystery surrounding the Capstone is a series of short verses in Zechariah that act like the hub of a large wheel. All references to this mysterious stone, throughout Scripture, revolve around this passage.

In it, the prophet subtly presents the victory of the forces of righteousness over the powers and principalities of the satanic kingdom of Babel. In a few short lines, Zechariah provides an incredible overview of the completed history of mankind.

ZECHARIAH 4

6 So he said to me, "This is the word of the LORD to Zerubbabel: 'Not by might nor by power, but by my Spirit,' says the LORD Almighty.

7 "What are you, O mighty mountain? Before Zerubbabel you will become level ground. Then he will bring out the capstone to shouts of 'God bless it! God bless it!'"

8 Then the word of the LORD came to me:

9 "The hands of Zerubbabel have laid the foundation of this temple; his hands will also complete it. Then you will know that the LORD Almighty has sent me to you."

The sign to all that the satanic kingdom on earth is destroyed is the presentation of a "capstone." This suggests that this one stone holds great significance to God and His future plans for mankind. The moment of its arrival will be the culmination of world history, a final deliverance for God's people on earth. Its appearance will be accompanied by great celebration and shouts of joy, "God Bless It!"

To see beyond the somewhat vague English translation of "capstone," it is necessary to look at the underlying Hebrew text. The Hebrew word for this stone is **Ro'sh 'eben**, where *'eben* is the Hebrew word for stone, and *Ro'sh* designates the kind of stone being described.[16] And this specific descriptive word acts like a lightning rod for the mystery laid out before us. **Ro'sh** has a series of definitions that, when taken together, provide an in-depth picture of this mysterious stone.

Ro'sh
the Head, the Highest Rank, our Captain, our Chief, The End, Excellent, the Highest Part, the Principal of All, the Ruler of All, the Sum of All Things, the Top of All Things[17]

Scripture elsewhere provides a physical demonstration of the concept behind this word **Ro'sh**. The word is used to describe the summits or peaks of mountains in various passages in the Bible, such as Genesis 8:5, Numbers 14:40 and Isaiah 42:11.

Zechariah implies at the end of this key passage that the capstone will be the one and only stone needed to finish the temple of the Messiah, Jesus as Zerub-Babel. This temple, as previously noted, is a spiritual, worldwide house of God representing the Church, the *righteous* Tower of Babel. It will be the place of gathering and unity for all peoples of the earth.

The Capstone Psalm
The author of Psalm 118 describes a day of great rejoicing and elation, similar to Zechariah's description of celebration. In fact, this Psalm is an expanded version of Zechariah 4:6-9, and explains in more detail the events taking place in Zechariah's core passage.

First, the same kind of shouts of joy and elation that were described by Zechariah are present in this Psalm.

Ps 118:15-16
Shouts of joy and victory resound in the tents of the righteous: "The LORD's right hand has done mighty things! The LORD's right hand is lifted high; the LORD's right hand has done mighty things!"

Second, we see the same word, "capstone," representing the reason for this joy and celebration.

Ps 118:22-24
The stone the builders rejected has become the **capstone** (*ro'sh pinnah*); the LORD has done this, and it is marvelous in our eyes. This is the day the LORD has made; **let us rejoice and be glad in it**.

Furthermore, we learn in this Psalm that the stone is at first rejected. Then in a wonderful sense of irony, the stone that was despised has become a triumphant and elevated stone, and this event will be "marvelous in our eyes." The stone has somehow been transformed from the lowest and rejected of stones to the most exalted and praised of stones, and is referred to, again, as a "capstone."

The Hebrew words chosen by the Psalmist to describe this stone are essentially the same as those used by Zechariah, except that an additional descriptive adjective is applied, **ro'sh** *pinnah*. We have already seen the definition of **ro'sh**. Now let's turn our attention to **pinnah**.

Pinnah is traditionally translated as "angle," although this greatly understates its true meaning. The more complete definition includes "pinnacle." It appears that the two words, **pinnah** and **pinnacle**, are related and even share the same etymological root. And this Hebrew word has specific relevance for our understanding of the mysterious stone.

As defined by *The American Heritage Dictionary*, a **pinnacle** is "a tall, pointed formation, such as a mountain peak" and "the highest point; summit; acme."[18] There is familiar language at work here. As with Zechariah's word **"ro'sh,"** we again encounter a Hebrew word that refers to the top of a mountain. In addition, the Psalmist appears to be over-emphasizing the point so that his readers do not miss it. The stone is both the **ro'sh** (the highest of all) and **pinnah** (the pinnacle of all), and *both* words have in their definition the "peak" of a mountain.

Isaiah Speaks of Stones

Next we turn to Isaiah. By analyzing this prophet's choice of words, we find that Isaiah has much to reveal.

Isa 28:16
"Behold, I lay in Zion for a foundation a stone, a tried stone, a precious **cornerstone** (*pinat*)..." (KJV)

The Lord, speaking through Isaiah, uses the word **pinat** to describe this stone, which is simply another form of the word **pinnah**. By this choice of words, He is implying that He is envisioning a mountain peak or summit. This leads us to a new perspective on this familiar passage from Isaiah. **The conclusion is that Isaiah's *cornerstone* is the same as the *capstone* found in Psalms and Zechariah.** These two terms in English appear differently but are, in reality, describing the same stone in the underlying Hebrew.

Notice, as well, the similarity in the condition of this stone. In the previous passage in Psalms, the stone was rejected by men, and yet exalted in the end. Here in Isaiah, the stone is tried and tested, and it is found to be precious. The high value placed on it comes, in part, from its trial and refinement as if by fire. And this implies that the stone has been through a great testing and has been found worthy.

A Specific Stone in God's House

In Ephesians, Paul describes the house of God. He presents a spiritual building, a house or temple, made up of stones representing believers. And Jesus, Paul notes, represents the most important stone in the house, the *chief cornerstone*. In Him, the entire building is joined together and rises to become the holy temple of the Lord.

Eph 2:19-22

Consequently, you are no longer foreigners and aliens, but fellow citizens with God's people and members of God's household, built on the foundation of the apostles and prophets, with Christ Jesus himself as the **chief cornerstone**. In him the whole building is joined together and rises to become a holy temple in the Lord. And in him you too are being built together to become a dwelling in which God lives by his Spirit.

The *chief cornerstone*, like the "cornerstone," has been interpreted as the most important stone at the foundation or base of a building, otherwise known as "the foundation stone." This image certainly fits with our knowledge of Jesus as the foundation of our faith. But as we will see, it does not fit in the context and language regarding this particular stone in Ephesians.

The Greek word Paul uses to describe the chief cornerstone is an important clue in the picture that is emerging. The word is "**akrogooniaíou**" and is constructed of two separate root words, **akron** and **gonia**.

The first, **akron**, is defined as "the extreme end, or top most, or utmost." It is the root word from which we get *acrophobia*, the fear of high places or the fear of heights. It is also the root word for *acropolis*, or the high, fortified center of cities in ancient Greece. As well, it is the root for the word *acrobat*, or those who sail upwards through the air. And it is the reason why there is a town named *Akron* in Ohio, the highest point in the surrounding terrain.

The intent here, certainly, cannot be to describe a stone at the base of a building. There is a clear reference to a stone *at considerable height*.

It is true that a stone at the base of a building often has more symbolic importance than other stones, the reason being that one stone is used to represent the entire foundation and integrity of a building. This is why most interpretations of this scripture have looked at the base of the building for the "most important" or chief cornerstone. In a pure architectural sense, however, no single stone at the corner of the base of a building is more important than any other. *Without stability on all four corners the building would collapse!* The analogy of a "chief" cornerstone simply does not apply to the base of a building, especially when we consider the root word **akron**.

The second Hebrew word, **gonia,** is defined as "angle" or "corner." When combined, **akrogooniaíou** forms the concept of utmost, topmost, or highest cornerstone.

The identity of Paul's highest, angular stone, which he calls the *chief cornerstone*, equates the stone to the same image found in Isaiah, the Psalms, and Zechariah. All of these stones represent Jesus, and all of these stones are found at the top of buildings or mountains. As with Isaiah and his Hebrew word **pinnah**, and Zechariah with his word **ro'sh**, we have Paul and his Greek word **akron**.

This leads us to a further conclusion. The **cornerstone,** the **chief cornerstone,** and the **capstone** are all the *same stone.* In various passages of Scripture, Hebrew words are translated differently in English, but they are referring to the same underlying image.

Peter Also Speaks of the Capstone

Peter, or Pétros (the rock), provides another key to unlock the Capstone Mystery. He builds his message in Greek using the Hebrew text from Isaiah 28:16, analyzed above. And he uses two words to describe this stone. The wording Peter uses, and the textual parallels to the Hebrew words in Isaiah 28, help to reveal the nature of the stone he is describing.

Before us stands a spiritual temple comprised of believers who are "living stones."

1 Peter 2:4-8

4   As you come to him, **the living Stone**—rejected by men but chosen by God and precious to him—

5   you also, like **living stones**, are being built into a spiritual house to be a holy priesthood, offering spiritual sacrifices acceptable to God through Jesus Christ.

6   For in Scripture it says:
> "See, I lay a stone in Zion, a chosen and precious **cornerstone** (*akrogooniaíou*), and the one who trusts in him will never be put to shame."

7   Now to you who believe, this stone is precious. But to those who do not believe,
> "The stone the builders rejected has become the **capstone** (*kefaleén goonías*)"

Peter begins by describing Jesus as the *Living Stone*. This is the state of Jesus now, in heaven, at the right hand of the throne of God. He has been tried and tested in the furnace of affliction, crushed for our transgressions, and has died for us on the cross of shame. Three days following His death, He rose from the dead, and prepared a way for us to follow in His victory over death. He then ascended to the throne in heaven, where He is alive and still interceding for us today.

Through the power and the might of the Holy Spirit, mankind is able to become like Jesus, and those who are born again by this Spirit become *living stones*. The stones that Peter is referring to are, therefore, eternally living stones, or lives in the eternal kingdom of God. And they are being built together into a spiritual house that will serve the Lord, forever. As such, these stones represent men and women in service to God, a holy priesthood, and they offer spiritual sacrifices in this righteous temple or tower of Zerub-Babel.

When Peter refers to the *cornerstone*, he is using the same word as Paul, **akrogooniaíou,** implying a stone at some height. In addition, Peter sources this quote directly from

Isaiah 28:16, and Isaiah, we noted, used the word **pinnah**
(*pinat*) when describing the cornerstone in his passage. This
quote of Peter's in the New Testament parallels the words
of Isaiah in the Old Testament, and equates the Hebrew word
pinnah with the Greek word **akrogooniaíou**! And **pinnah**
is the same as **pinnacle**, which we saw defined as the peak
or summit of a mountain.

Peter has just provided a direct link between his stone,
Paul's stone in Ephesians, and the *pinnacle stone* in Isaiah.
Paul and Peter have now joined the ranks of other Biblical
authors who refer to Jesus as a stone and as a mountain
summit or peak.

Further in this passage, Peter calls the same stone by a
different name. This time he references the Capstone Psalm,
Psalm 118, when he says that the "stone the builders rejected
has become the capstone." He uses two words to describe
this stone, "**kefaleén goonías**." The first translates into the
"head" as in the uppermost part of the body, and the second
translates as "corner" as in angle or edge. The head is at the
top of the body, and in fact is the highest point in the human
form. Thus this stone is at the head, and the highest point, of
the Lord's temple (or house).

As mentioned, Peter is referencing an Old Testament
source. The **ro'sh pinnah** of Psalm 118:22 is the same as the
kefaleén goonías of 1 Peter 2:7. And the pinnacle stone of
the Psalmist is the same as the capstone of Peter.

The terms Peter chooses to describe this stone are directly
related to the *cornerstone* from Isaiah and the *capstone* from
the Psalmist. And his words in Greek are entirely consistent
with the definitions of the Hebrew words we have found so
far. In addition, there is an obvious relationship between
Peter's "head of the body" and Zechariah's "head of the
mountain."

Viewed All at Once

Combining the above references to this stone into a
comparative chart allows us a view of the larger picture
which is emerging.

References to
The Mysterious Capstone

Zech. 4:7
ro'sh 'eben
Head Stone, Highest Stone, Chief Stone,
the Highest Part, Sum of All, Top of All

Hebrew Text   *Greek Text*

Ps. 118:22
ro'sh pinnah
The Pinnacle Stone, as in
Mountain Peak or Summit

1st Peter 2:7
kefaleén goonías
Head Stone of the Corner,
or Top Angled Stone

Sourced

Is. 28:16
pinat
The Pinnacle Stone,
as in Mountain Peak or Summit

1 Peter 2:6
akrogooniaíou
The Highest Angled Stone,
or 'Chief Cornerstone'
Also **Ephesians 2:20**

Sourced

Zechariah represents the beginning point in the understanding of the meaning behind this stone. The Psalmist follows, and is directly quoted by Peter. Isaiah then presents his version, and is directly quoted by Peter as well.

When combining all of these descriptions of the capstone, we begin to envision Zerub-Babel's temple with a crowning capstone, a stone in the shape of a mountain peak. Using simple deduction, we can suggest:

Where there is a mountain peak, there is most likely a mountain underneath

The presence of the capstone in Scripture begins to act like a suggestive tool that prompts us to conclude "wherever you see a capstone, there is a mountain close at hand." The mountain is not like mountains we know, made up of solid rock or earth, for it is a temple, and its peak is a stone. According to Peter, this temple is made up of living stones and the highest stone is the Living Stone, Jesus Christ.

The Mist Finally Clears:
Envisioning the Mysterious Peak

The relationships are consistent. The imagery is clear. Yet questions remain. Are we looking at the same building from different angles? And will one stone meet all the necessary criteria?

There is only one building that fits the description of a mountain. It so happens that this same building is also known for its spiritual nature, as a form of a temple. While it is comprised of stones, it has a single, angular cornerstone at the top, which in its architectural role caps the temple like a mountain peak.

And this building or temple is the **Pyramid**.

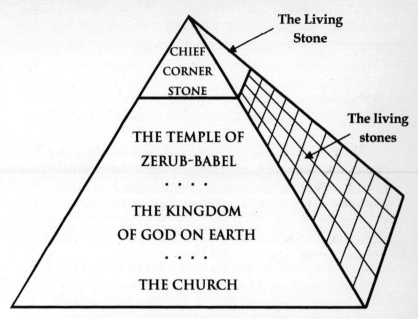

The Chosen Design for the Temple of the Messiah

The kingdom of God on earth is described by Peter as a holy nation of saints. This nation is actually a spiritual kingdom, and it is being compared to a *temple* of God, His new covenant Church. This is a temple whose foundation stone was laid two thousand years ago when Jesus died on the cross. As with the previous temples of the Old Covenant, this temple is also the *spiritual house* of God, the place of His Spirit's *dwelling*, and the *tabernacle* of the New Covenant. And all these elements are brought together in the image of a **mountain of living stones**, through the words of Peter, Paul, the Psalmist, Isaiah and Zechariah. The final stone in this building, the point of completion, is the Living Stone, the **capstone**, and this will be Jesus Christ when He returns at the end of the age. He will emerge, as Zechariah says, to shouts of celebration and "God Bless It!"

At the top of this mountain, like any mountain we see on earth, is a summit, the "peak." This is Jesus (1 Peter 2:4).

At the top of the temple of Zerub-Babel is the Capstone, and
that is Jesus (Zech. 4:7). At the top of the Body of Christ (the
Church) is the head, and that is again Jesus (Eph 1:22, Rom
12:4-5). Standing in authority over the household and the
Bride is the Husband and that is, yet again, Jesus (1 Peter
3:1). Above the earth and throughout heaven there is one
Lord of Lords, and one King of Kings, and that, too, is Jesus
(Eph 1:10).

The Rock at the summit of this temple mountain is the
living Stone, the resurrected Messiah enthroned on high. This
is the Rock that is referred to as our fortress and deliverer,
our refuge and shield, our stronghold and the horn of our
salvation.

Ps 18:2

The LORD is my rock, my **fortress** and my
deliverer; my God is my rock, in whom I take
refuge. He is my **shield** and **the horn of my
salvation**, my **stronghold**.

During the Old Covenant, God chose to dwell on the
summit of the Temple Mount in Jerusalem, and in the
innermost room of the Temple, known as the Holiest of
Holies. This is where the Ark of the Covenant was placed,
along with the accompanying Mercy Seat. This throne was
situated, by God's design, at the highest point on Mount Zion,
and was the throne of God on earth. It was also a mirror of
the arrangement of the throne of God in heaven, on the
"utmost heights of the sacred mountain." And so, the Lord's
throne in heaven had a counterpart in the world below. In
heaven, as on earth, God ruled from the **summit of a holy
mount**.

Under the New Covenant, the Lord's dwelling in heaven
is still on the utmost heights of a sacred mountain, the same
magnificent mountain as before. His dwelling on earth,
however, *has changed*. It is still on a mount or mountain, but
a very different mountain from before. **This time, His earthly
dwelling is on a spiritual mountain.** And this spiritual
mountain is also a temple, the Temple of Zerub-Babel, and
the righteous Tower of Babel that Zechariah has described.

It is the place of the dwelling of His Holy Spirit, and it is through this temple that the Spirit's power and might are being demonstrated. It is the new house of God, the members of which are the "living stones" and they are united as one in the family of Christ.

The throne of God under the Old Covenant, the Ark of the Covenant, was placed at the summit of the "Temple Mount." The Ark has been replaced by a new throne of God, on the summit of a "Temple Mountain." The physical *Mount Zion* is replaced by a far greater, spiritual *Mountain of Zion*. And the capstone represents the most exalted place on the mountain, the highest honor, the crown. On this spiritual mountain, the capstone is placed at the summit, and therefore represents the *throne of God on earth*.

Through the discovery of this mountain of stones and the nature of its crowning capstone, we also come to the meaning behind the image of the altars built by patriarchs, dating back to the earliest worship of God. These rough altars built by Noah, Abraham, Jacob, and others were pointing to a much greater altar, or mountain of stone, that was to come. They were the archetypes of the coming temple and mountain of Zerub-Babel, the Mountain of Zion, the symbol for the kingdom of God on earth. At the summit resides the throne of the Messiah of all mankind.

Zechariah's Epic Battle

With the shape and position of the capstone revealed, we now have the missing piece to the interpretation of Zechariah. It is worth returning again to the core of the capstone mystery, where the journey began. And this time we find ourselves in the midst of a battle of epic proportions.

ZECHARIAH 4

6 So he said to me, "This is the word of the LORD to Zerubbabel: 'Not by might nor by power, but by my Spirit,' says the LORD Almighty.

7 "What are you, O mighty mountain? Before Zerubbabel you will become level ground. Then he will bring out the capstone to shouts of 'God bless it! God bless it!'"

8   Then the word of the LORD came to me:

9   "The hands of Zerubbabel have laid the foundation
       of this temple; his hands will also complete it. Then
       you will know that the LORD Almighty has sent
       me to you."

Zechariah is telling us, through the use of contrasting
language, that there are actually *two mountains* present! The
first mountain is the "mighty mountain" that represents the
satanic kingdom on earth, and is essentially a spiritual
building project that began following the first Tower of Babel.
This "spiritual Babel" continues to represent the rebellion
against God by the elite among man, even today. This
mountain will be leveled, completely defeated, and will be
replaced by a second, far greater mountain.

The presence of the second mountain is implied through
the mention of the *capstone*. This triumphant stone, the **ro'sh**,
or as the Psalmist says "the **ro'sh pinnah**," is in the shape of
a mountain peak. And as logic tells us, where there is a
mountain peak, there is a mountain underneath. The
Capstone reveals a second mountain, one that is in contrast
to the mighty mountain. This second mountain will be
victorious over the first mountain, and will be the completed
temple of Zerub-Babel, which is the new covenant Church
founded by Jesus Christ. For the purposes of contrast, it is
also referred to, in this book, as the *righteous* Tower of Babel,
as it counters the "mighty mountain" that is an image of the
original Tower of Babel. Furthermore, it destroys the effects
of Babel, and unites the followers of Christ into one nation
and one tongue.

Zerub-Babel, as Zechariah says, is the one who laid the
first stone for this pyramidal, mountain of stones. Zerub-
Babel will also be the one to place the final stone, the
capstone, on its peak. This finishing stone is the Living Stone,
and will represent the coming of the Messiah at the
completion of the kingdom of God on earth. Appropriately,
it will be brought out to great shouts of joy in a victory
celebration.

Z4:7   "Then he will bring out the *capstone* to shouts of **'God bless it! God bless it!'**"

The last two thousand years have witnessed simultaneous, massive construction projects for two very different towers. One tower, Babel —the tower of man's might or the mighty mountain — is a growing, worldwide rebellion to the true God and His destiny for mankind. It will be destroyed in the last days. The other Tower — the mountain of the Lord's might — represents God's will for unity, peace, and salvation for mankind, available only through the shed blood of His Son, the Messiah. This mountain will be victorious in leveling the first and will become established with even greater heights. Zechariah tells us how the mountain of evil is to be destroyed.

Z4:6   'Not by might nor by power, **but by my Spirit**,' says the LORD Almighty.

The mighty mountain represents the counterfeit kingdom on earth and is a temple and house of that false god, Lucifer. And this mountain temple is also a **pyramid**. For confirmation of this we turn to the prophet Jeremiah. When he refers to the destroying mountain of the satanic kingdom on earth, he includes descriptive elements that prove, beyond a shadow of doubt, that Satan's temple is also a mountain of stones, or pyramid.

Jer 51:26
"I am against you, **O destroying mountain**, you who destroy the whole earth," declares the LORD. No rock will be taken from you for a **cornerstone** (*pinnah*), nor any stone for a **foundation** (*yoceed*), for you will be desolate forever"

This mighty, destroying mountain has two specific stones to offer the kingdom of God, a foundation stone and a pinnacle stone. A mountain that has a foundation stone and a pinnacle stone is a *pyramid*. Neither stone, however, will be taken by God, and the mountain of Satan's throne will instead be leveled, left desolate forever. Only the true Messiah, Jesus Christ, will be the foundation and chief cornerstone of the New Covenant and the worldwide temple of God!

The Clash of Two Mountains

Zechariah allows us to compare these two mountains side by side. On the one hand we have a glorious mountain, the spiritual temple of Zerub-Babel, the throne of God. On the other hand we have an occult, dark mountain, which is the spiritual temple of Satan's evil on earth.

> ➢ If Zerub-Babel's temple is in the shape of a mountain, so Babel's temple is in the shape of a mountain (the "mighty mountain").

> ➢ If Zerub-Babel's temple is in fact a pyramid, then Babel's temple is also a pyramid.

> ➢ If the mountain under construction by Zerub-Babel is made up of stones, referred to by Peter as *living stones*, then the mountain of spiritual Babel is also made up of stones, although these are *dead stones*.

> ➢ If the sign of completion of Zerub-Babel's temple is the crowning of a capstone, then the sign of completion of Babel's temple will also be in the form of a capstone. The capstone has the same architectural role in both temples.

> ➢ If Zerub-Babel's temple is a house and the place of God's dwelling, then Babel's temple will also be a house and a place of dwelling for the doomed prince, the false god of this world, Satan or Lucifer.

This is all in accordance with a principle known as "counterfeit." We find ourselves looking at two very similar objects, one as the original and one as the reverse, like a reflection in a distorted mirror.

Clearly, we cannot underestimate the extent to which Lucifer (the thief) has stolen the most powerful images he once saw in heaven, and has used them to establish his own kingdom on earth, ever since his rebellion and fall. There has always been a strong indication that the things of God have been stolen and corrupted in the kingdom of Satan. It would appear that he faced the glorious heights of the sacred mountain in heaven on a daily basis, and in his heart lusted after its possession, especially the throne. And he uses counterfeit versions of these marvelous things to entrap mankind to this day.

Isa 14:12-13
You (Lucifer) said in your heart, "I will ascend to heaven; I will raise my throne above the stars of God; **I will sit enthroned on the mount of assembly,** on the **utmost heights of the sacred mountain.**"

This mirroring of the sacred things in heaven is a powerful tool in Satan's kingdom, and will be explained in more detail. For the time being, it is worth noting that the world is filled with images of the counterfeit kingdom of God, temples in the shape of pyramids!

Revisiting Paul in Ephesians
In Ephesians, Paul describes exactly what we have seen through Peter, a spiritual building composed of living stones with Jesus as the Chief Cornerstone. And his description of the house of God fits the image of the pyramid quite well!

Eph 2:19-22
Consequently, you are no longer foreigners and aliens, but fellow citizens with God's people and members of God's household...with Christ Jesus himself as the **chief cornerstone. In him the whole building is** *joined together* **and rises** to become a holy temple in the Lord. And in him you too are being built together to become a dwelling in which God lives by his Spirit.

Paul says that in Jesus, the whole building is *joined together*. This is precisely the architectural role of the capstone; it is the one and only point of unison in the entire mountain of stones. This building, Paul states, rises (presumably at an angle) to become the holy temple of the Lord.

Paul's use of the word "rises" has two meanings here. In the King James Version, it is rendered "groweth." In Greek, it is **aúxei,** and it means "to enlarge" and "to increase." First, the passage implies that the mountain rises before us visually, in the sense of it being tall or of considerable height. Second, it implies that this is a living mountain, a mountain that is enlarging or growing. How does this living mountain grow? When new, living stones are added to it. Each time someone accepts Jesus, this mountain gains another stone!

Paul places Jesus Christ in the position of the Chief Cornerstone, as Lord of Lords and King of Kings. This is echoed by Paul elsewhere, in Ephesians:

Eph 1:9-10
...to be put into effect when the times will have reached their fulfillment—**to bring all things in heaven and on earth together under one head, even Christ**.

All things in heaven and on earth will one day be brought under one head(stone), and that head is the Messiah Jesus Christ.

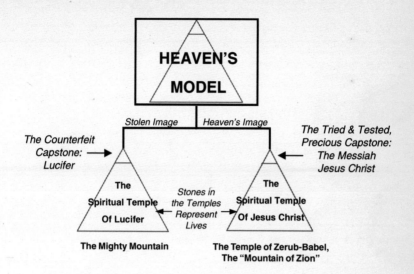

7

CONFIRMATIONS

There are a number of artifacts, including drawings, diagrams, and monuments that support the solution to the capstone mystery. Some of these artifacts are surprisingly part of everyday life in the world around us, others are hidden away by divine instruction. All of them, though, are exciting confirmations of what is being revealed here, and prompt us to delve further into the rich meaning behind this living Stone.

Individually these confirmations provide assurances that the new, spiritual temple of Jesus Christ is in the shape of a mountain of stones, a pyramid. Collectively, they provide strong evidence that this specific image was, first and foremost, the design by God for His kingdom in heaven, and now serves as the blueprint for the kingdom being built on earth. They assure us that we are witnessing the realization of God's will as declared in the Lord's prayer: "on earth as it is in heaven."

As before, we begin with the prophet Zechariah.

Confirmation #1
The Tomb of the Capstone Prophet

Because of the prophet's numerous references to the stone in question, Zechariah earns the title of the *capstone prophet*. As mentioned, the fourth chapter of Zechariah acts like the "center of a wheel" for all the prophetic references to the return of Jesus Christ. In addition, the fourth chapter is also a beginning point on the journey to better understand the image of the capstone in the Bible. There are at least two additional references to the capstone in the relatively few chapters of the book of Zechariah.

The second reference occurs in his tenth chapter.

Zech 10:3-5
From Judah will come the cornerstone (*pinnah*)

This is a vision of Jesus, who through Mary and, by adoption, Joseph is descended through the bloodline of King David and is thus of the tribe of Judah. We understand from Zechariah and others that the Messiah was also to be a greater version of Solomon and Zerubbabel, both of whom are also of the Davidic bloodline. It is in this line of descent that we find two characteristics of the Messiah: king and *temple builder*.

As with Isaiah and the Psalmist, the word Zechariah uses in this verse for the cornerstone is **pinnah**, or pinnacle. And pinnacle, as we saw earlier, is defined as the mountain peak, or summit. Like the first reference to the capstone in the book of Zechariah, the second reference confirms the image of the stone as a mountain peak.

The Capstone Prophet's Tomb

Just outside the walls of the original city of Jerusalem, at the base of the eastern side of the Temple Mount, is the Kidron Valley. This valley is roughly three miles in length, and extends beyond the Mount of Olives. It is mentioned eleven times in the Old and New Testament, and is also referred to as the Valley of the Kings, and as the Valley of Jehoshaphat.

Jesus would have crossed the Kidron on his way to Gethsemane, at the foot of the Mount of Olives.

John 18:1
When he had finished praying, Jesus left with his disciples and crossed the **Kidron Valley**.

Carved out of the rock face on a mountainside in the Kidron Valley is the tomb of the prophet Zechariah. It stands over ten meters tall, and was constructed during the Second Temple period.[19]

At Zechariah's tomb we find a visual confirmation of the meaning behind his words. The shape of the prophet's tomb is striking and specific, unique in design. It is the only tomb shaped like a **pyramid capstone** in the entire King's Valley in Jerusalem!

Adam Rutherford, 20th century scholar of the messianic nature of pyramids in Egypt, states:

> "This mausoleum of Zechariah crowned with a pyramid (capstone) is still to be seen at the present day in Jerusalem. It is situated in the rocky Valley of Jehoshaphat, between the ancient Temple area and the Mount of Olives. In that great valley of graves, no other sepulchral monument is crowned with a pyramid."[20]

Zechariah's Tomb in the Kidron Valley, Jerusalem

Very few people know that there is a pyramid in Israel. And what better place to find it than at the tomb of the capstone prophet!

The entire tomb is carved from the rock face and is, as such, a single stone. This is not by accident, as this characteristic demonstrates the words of Zechariah. Throughout his book the prophet presents two aspects of the Messiah together, side-by-side: the servant and the king. They are to him, inextricable. In addition, the laying of the foundation and the presentation of the capstone, both by Zerub-Babel, are part of a continuous action, and are performed by the same person. Thus from the foundation up to the capstone, the prophet's tomb is of one stone, and represents one statement, one action.

Furthermore, as the photograph shows, there is a strong, visual characteristic in the symbol of the capstone. It is found in the stone's razor-sharp edges. The top stone of a pyramid, the capstone, is actually referred to as a pyramidion; it is a smaller model of an overall pyramid. The top of Zechariah's tomb is a perfectly carved pyramidion, while the presence of a much larger pyramid is suggested as the eye follows the lines formed by the angles of that top stone. This is an excellent visual example that demonstrates the simple, logical conclusion that "where there is a mountain peak, there is a reference to a larger mountain underneath." This statement can be revised as "where there is a capstone (pyramidion) there is a reference to a larger pyramid underneath."

It would be inconceivable to imagine, in the perfect wisdom of God, a top stone in the shape of a mountain peak chosen as the most exalted stone of His kingdom, while the building underneath presents disharmony to this stone in any manner or form. **The Godly capstone, as the head, forms perfect unity with the rest of the building, or body, beneath.** Why else would God choose a top stone in the shape of a mountain peak unless there was supposed to be a mountain underneath? There cannot be even a hint of disunity in the temple under construction by Zerub-Babel; it will be absolutely perfect in unity and in design. In the case of the tomb, we find that the foundation is also in the shape of a pyramid, as a series of steps. And so the top of the tomb, as well as the base of the tomb, refer to the same overall image, the mountain referred to as Zerub-Babel's temple.

The presence of the capstone at the tomb of Zechariah may also explain the misguided expectations of the nation of Israel leading up to the life and ministry of Jesus. The chief priests and Pharisees were looking for a crowned king, a finishing capstone, and did not expect the humble, suffering servant, who came as the foundation stone. They were unable to understand the seemingly contradictory references to a Messiah who was to be "wounded for our transgressions," but at the same time would "judge between the nations." Indeed, they were expecting the King described in Zechariah 9:10 instead of the One portrayed in Zechariah 9:9.

Zech 9:10
His rule will extend from sea to sea and from the River **to the ends of the earth**.

Zech 9:9
See, your king comes to you, righteous and having salvation, **gentle** and **riding on a donkey**, on a colt, the foal of a donkey.

Many, so it seems, have tried to discredit the prophet Zechariah, and have sought to disconnect his name from this tomb. The revelation of the capstone, however, confirms that the name attributed to the tomb is correct, that name being Zechariah, the *"capstone prophet."* At the very least, the capstone logically dictates for whom this monument was dedicated, if the prophet is indeed buried elsewhere.

Confirmation #2
John Envisions a Mountain Great and High
In the last pages of the Book of Revelation, the Apostle John is given a revelation of a bride beautifully dressed for her husband. The bride refers to the followers of Christ, who are presented throughout Scripture as the "Bride of Christ." John explains this revelation in terms of a vision, in which he describes a mountain both great and high.

Rev 21:9-11

One of the seven angels who had the seven bowls full of the seven last plagues came and said to me, "Come, I will show you **the bride**, the wife of the Lamb." And he carried me away in the Spirit to **a mountain great and high**, and showed me the **Holy City**, **Jerusalem**, coming down out of heaven from God.

The passage implies that the *mountain great and high* and the *wife of the Lamb* are **the same**! This mountain is the future kingdom of God, also referred to as the Holy City of Jerusalem and the "Bride." It is the main city of the new heavens and new earth, far in the future. However, given what we know so far, this high mountain is related to the completed Temple of Zerub-Babel, over which Jesus is Lord and Head. It is a reflection of the *righteous* Tower of Babel, the tower being built by Jesus Christ in order to unite redeemed man into one nation and tongue.

Later in the same passage, John notes some of the dimensions of this Holy City, this mountain great and high:

Rev 21:15-16

The angel who talked with me had a measuring rod of gold to measure the city, its gates and its walls. The city was laid out like a square, **as long as it was wide**.

At its base, the city is laid out "like a square." This defines the base or the foundation of a pyramid, which has four sides of equal length. Perhaps this is a symbolic reminder to citizens of this kingdom that Jesus is the perfect foundation of their faith. As one would expect from the dimensions of a square, the city is "as long as it is wide."

Then, John provides us with more information about this mountain, the *height*.

Rev 21:16

He measured the city with the rod and found it to be 12,000 stadia in length, **and as wide and high as it is long**.

The city is *as tall* as it is long and wide. This tells us that the pinnacle of the mountain is as high, vertically, as any one of the sides of the base is long or wide, horizontally.

This is architectural purity and divine harmony at work, with the Bride of Christ in the shape of a beautifully proportioned mountain.

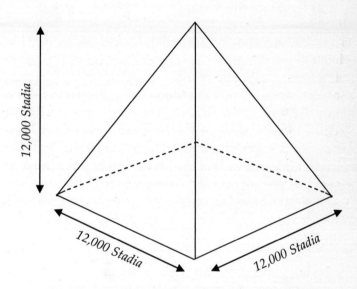

The New City of Jerusalem, Far in the Future

Confirmation #3
The Stone with Eyes

Returning to the book of Zechariah, there is yet another mention of the capstone, the third reference from this prophet so far. With this reference we find another confirmation of the solution to the age-old mystery surrounding this stone.

This time the Stone is found in the third chapter, a brief selection that is heavy with prophetic imagery. The relevant passage is Zechariah 3: 8–10; and here we learn many things.

Zech 3:8-10

"'Listen, O high priest Joshua and your associates seated before you, who are men symbolic of things to come: I am going to bring my servant, **the Branch**. See, **the stone** I have set in front of Joshua! **There are seven eyes on that one stone**, and I will engrave an inscription on it,' says the LORD Almighty, 'and I will remove the sin of this land in a single day.'"

First, we learn that Joshua and the associates around him are symbolic of things in the future. Zerubbabel (or Zerub-Babel) was no doubt one of those associates.

Second, we learn that the **Stone** being placed in front of Joshua *is the same as the* **Branch**. The Stone and the Branch are both representative of the Messiah, Jesus Christ. For instance, Jesus is prophetically referred to as the *Branch* in Isaiah, who informs us that the Messiah is to have the *seven Spirits of God* resting on Him. These seven spirits consist of six unique aspects and an overarching Spirit as the seventh, the Holy Spirit.

Isa 11:1-3

A shoot will come up from the stump of Jesse; from his roots a **Branch** will bear fruit. **The Spirit of the LORD** will rest on him — the Spirit of **wisdom** and of **understanding**, the Spirit of **counsel** and of **power**, the Spirit of **knowledge** and of the **fear** of the LORD— and he will delight in the fear of the LORD.

Third, we learn from Zechariah 3:8 that the Lord will "remove the sin of this land" in a single day, as a foreshadowing of the sacrificial work of the Messiah on the cross.

Finally, we learn from Zechariah that this stone has *eyes*. And not just one eye, but in fact *seven eyes*. As we are told in the next chapter of Zechariah, the infamous fourth chapter:

Zech 4:10
"These seven are the eyes of the LORD, which range throughout the earth."

Jesus is presented as a *stone with seven eyes*, a here-to-fore undisclosed image of the Messiah! Most would suggest that this is an odd, if not uncomfortable, way to picture the Son of God. There are images of Jesus with which we have a degree of comfort, including the Branch and the Lamb, images that are widely recognized and discussed. **But a stone with seven eyes is a completely new revelation of Jesus Christ to the modern Church!** And so the question arises, does this image appear elsewhere in Scripture?

It most certainly does. This is an image of the Messiah described in John's vision of heaven in the Book of Revelation, where he sees a Lamb at the throne.

Rev 5:6
"Then I saw a Lamb, looking as if it had been slain, standing in the center of the throne, encircled by the four living creatures and the elders. He had seven horns and **seven eyes, which are the seven spirits of God sent out into all the earth."**

This Lamb that was slain, Jesus Christ, has seven eyes that are "sent throughout the earth," just as the Stone has seven eyes that "range throughout the earth."

And so, three images of Jesus have just been miraculously equated. The *Branch* is the same as the *Stone*, courtesy of Zechariah 3:8, and the *Stone* is the same as the *Lamb that was slain*, as supported by the seven eyes in Revelation 5:6. The question remains, however, as to the precise meaning and nature of the seven eyes.

In the first chapter of the Book of Revelation, we find the answer. We learn that these seven eyes represent the *Holy Spirit*, the Spirit that bestows the power and authority of the Father, God Almighty. In the passage that follows, *all three members* of the trinity are presented:

Rev 1:4-5
"Grace and peace to you from him **who is, and who was, and who is to come** [*God the Father*], and from the **seven spirits** before his throne [*the Holy Spirit*], and from **Jesus Christ** [*Son of God*], who is the faithful witness, the firstborn from the dead, and the ruler of the kings of the earth."

Revelation 5:6 informs us that the seven eyes are the "seven spirits of God sent out into all the earth," and Revelation 1:4 reveals that the seven spirits are the third member of the Trinity, the Holy Spirit. The Holy Spirit is therefore being represented by seven eyes which in turn represent seven spirits. And this Spirit has come to rest on the Messiah, pictured as both a stone (Zechariah) and the Lamb that was slain (Revelation). This is the same Spirit that now empowers His body, the Church. For some divine purpose, the Holy Spirit has been divided into, or perhaps augmented with, six spirits that each ministers the will of God, plus the Holy Spirit itself as the seventh.

Notice that the seven eyes in Revelation rest on the Lamb *after it has been slain*, implying that this is an image of Jesus after His death and resurrection, and subsequent ascension to the heavenly throne. This is the Messiah in His post resurrection, exalted state. Additionally, the seven eyes rest on a stone, which should also be representative of Jesus in His post-resurrection, highly exalted state. According to the solution of the mystery in the preceding chapter, the highly exalted, post-resurrection form of Jesus Christ **is the pyramid capstone**. And so Jesus Christ is revealed in Zechariah as a *capstone with seven eyes*.

Yet is there any other evidence which would indicate the precise shape of the stone from Zechariah that has seven eyes? There is additional evidence of such, in the most unusual and unlikely of places. To see the answer firsthand, we must turn to a piece of evidence from everyday life, and an image that faces us on a daily basis. We turn to the United States' one-dollar bill.

When examining the back of the dollar you will see two

circular engravings. Each circle represents one side of the Great Seal of the United States, just like a coin with two sides…heads on the left, tails on the right. On the right you will see the eagle, and on the left, a pyramid.

The Great Seal of the United States

This pyramid has thirteen levels, and a capstone bathed in light. **Notice that the capstone on the left part of the seal has an eye!** This is clearly meant to represent a supernatural being of some kind. It is a capstone with one eye, as opposed to the capstone in Zechariah with seven eyes. This provides a strong indication that pyramid capstones represent supernatural beings, especially when adorned with eyes. And these elevated stones, when pictured with eyes, represent something of a *vastly important spiritual nature*.

What is the precise meaning of this capstone on the pyramid of the Great Seal, the capstone with an eye? Remember that in Zechariah there are **two mountains**, a mighty mountain of spiritual Babel and an even mightier mountain of Zerub-Babel. One is the unrighteous mountain or Tower that will unify man in rebellion to God in the last days, the "mighty mountain." This is the *second* or *figurative* Tower of Babel. And as shocking as this may be, this is what is pictured on the back of the U.S. currency! **The pyramid on the Great Seal is the spiritual Tower of Babel.** The capstone with the eye represents the image of *man enthroning man as God* at the summit, precisely what took place at the original Tower of Babel. This image will be explained in greater detail later, but for now it is worth pointing out that the top stone on the pyramid on the Great Seal is a symbol for a man enthroned as a *false messiah*, ruling over the entire earth.

The second mountain, the righteous tower of Zerub-Babel, is evidenced in Zechariah by the appearance of a *different capstone* (**ro'sh**) in the shape of a mountain peak. This is the true Messiah of the world, Jesus Christ. We have learned that this stone will have the seven eyes of the Holy Spirit. The true Messiah, Jesus, will return to destroy all the evil that this counterfeit mountain represents, and He will be the force who will dethrone the false messiah at the top. *The true Messiah will dethrone the false messiah*: this will be an enormous victory for the kingdom of God. The Lord's mountain will then become established as the worldwide, spiritual temple of man, with all races and peoples united under the global reign of Jesus Christ. And the righteous capstone will be brought out to shouts of celebration, "God Bless It!"

As we learn from Zechariah and Jeremiah, both mountains have capstones, and with the evidence of the Great Seal, both capstones have eyes! This is a perfect example of the **Principle of Counterfeit**, which has been mentioned before. What God created and designed for His purposes, Satan stole and tries to use for his own.

The crafters of the Great Seal created this image at the founding of the United States. They believed, however, that they were involved in much more than the founding of a single country. They saw themselves as creating a model for a global society, a model which the rest of the world could follow. We know this from their choice of the phrase "Novus Ordo Seclorum" borrowed from the Roman poet Virgil, the phrase that appears beneath the pyramid. It is translated as "New Order of the Ages" or more simply "New World Order."

Along these lines, these men were also one step away from enthroning man as God. Instead, they enthroned the *spirit of man*, the god of reason and enlightenment. This belief system is known as humanism. And the Great Seal with its supernatural capstone was the symbol they chose to mark the occasion. It was the sign of the creation of a new superpower that enthroned man, or man's own faculties of reason, as god for the entire world. There was neither the desire, nor the need, for the true Messiah Jesus Christ, in their plans of a global society.

Furthermore, there are obvious parallels to the first Tower of Babel where *man first enthroned man as God* at the summit of a tower or mountain.[21] That the crafters of the Great Seal chose the symbol of a tower, a "mighty mountain," for their global model of government is chilling. It appears that the Seal was part of a statement of occult prophecy regarding a coming new order or "age," that will unite the globe in harmony *without Jesus Christ*.

As incredible and disturbing as this all appears, there is no suggestion that the United States is evil. Rather, the Great Seal simply indicates that the forces of spiritual Babel have touched the American shores as they have *everywhere else on earth*. They, like Zerub-Babel, are involved in the creation of a worldwide spiritual temple of men, and quite naturally they included this newly created nation of the United States within their sights.

If the image of spiritual Babel is a pyramid, as suggested by Zechariah, Jeremiah, and now the Great Seal of the United States, does this not suggest that the original Tower of Babel was also in the shape of a pyramid? We will explore this next.

Confirmation #4
The First Migdal

The story behind this first attempt at a universal Tower occurs in Genesis, and includes a number of descriptive elements. For instance, the tower was made of white brick, perhaps as an outer covering, and the builders used bitumen (asphalt) instead of mortar. The Hebrew word used for the tower-building project is **migdal**. As the following verse relates:

Gen 11:4
"Come, let us build ourselves a city, with a **tower** [*migdal*] that reaches to the heavens, so that we may make a name for ourselves and not be scattered over the face of the whole earth."

The design of the Tower is not explicitly defined. However, there are enough implicit details to allow the reader to come to a conclusion, with a degree of certainty. For instance, an interesting detail emerges from the Hebrew definition of the word **migdal**, as found in *Strong's Concordance*:

Migdal
a tower (from its size or height); by analogy, a rostrum; figuratively, a (pyramidal) bed of flowers[22]

The description of a "pyramidal bed of flowers" implies that objects shaped like a pyramid were referred to as **migdals** including, oddly enough, beds of flowers. In addition to this clue, we are given a further nudge by the terminology used to describe the plan for the top of the Tower. The King James translation brings this out best:

Gen 11:4
And they said, Go to, let us build us a city and a tower, whose **top** (*ro'sh*) may reach unto heaven (KJV)

The word used to describe the top of the monument is the Hebrew word **ro'sh**! The meaning of this word had great significance when we analyzed the core passage in Zechariah. It is the Hebrew word often used in the Old Testament to designate mountain summits or mountain peaks. It also is *the same word* used to describe the pyramid capstone, or the peak of the mountain of stones, by both Zechariah and the Psalmist. The implication is that **the top of the tower was analogous to the summit of a mountain**.

In addition, we are told that the "head" of the tower was meant to "reach the heavens." However, the Hebrew text leaves out the verb. It literally reads "whose top...unto heaven." An alternative translation might be "whose top is like unto heaven," or even "whose top mirrors or reflects heaven." This introduces a new interpretation of the first Tower of Babel. It suggests that its top was meant to mirror, or to reflect, the throne of God in heaven, the throne that Isaiah told us resides on the utmost heights of the *sacred mountain*! And the throne we now know is the pinnacle or capstone.

The assumption here is not that all **migdals** are in the shape of mountains or pyramids; this is clearly not the case. Rather, pyramidal mountains or temples are a *specific form* of **migdal**, and this is what was built on the Plain of Shinar at the first tower project.

It is also a fascinating confirmation of the epic battle underway in Zechariah's core passage. The mighty, spiritual mountain of Babel will be leveled, implying that its **ro'sh** will be dethroned. The new mountain or tower of Zerub-Babel will then be established, and the true and righteous **Ro'sh** set on its throne. The word Genesis uses to describe the summit of the original Tower is the precise word Zechariah has used to describe the Messianic Capstone! Clearly there is a parallel being drawn to the original Tower of Babel by Zechariah in his core passage.

> **Z4:7** "What are you, O **mighty mountain**? Before Zerubbabel you will become level ground." Then he will bring out the **capstone** [*ro'sh*] to shouts of 'God bless it! God bless it!'"

Another descriptive source for the word **migdal** is *Vine's Expository Dictionary of Biblical Words*, which has a number of interesting translations. One that stands out is *watchtower*.[23] Significantly, we noted that Jacob built an altar in the shape of a heap or mound of stones, with a level platform at the top. And he named this mound Mizpah which means "watchtower" (Gen. 31:49). Furthermore, pyramids throughout the world were built to function as watchtowers. These mountains of stones were observatories for conducting astronomical calculations and measurements, for "watching" the heavens.

With the exception of Egypt, most of the pyramids left to us by older civilizations lack the crowning top stone, by design, creating the effect of a level platform at the summit. Given what we know about the meaning of the capstone, this would suggest ancient man was waiting for the return of a god or messiah to the earth. The level platform at the top of the pyramid was used, quite logically, to watch the heavens for signs of this god's return, and to communicate with him or her in the meantime.

Examples of this are found in Mexico City, at the Pyramids of the Sun and the Moon, and in Chichen Itza at the Temple of Kukulcan, in the Yucatan Peninsula. Even the large earth mountain known as Monk's Mound at Cahokia, in the Midwestern United States, has a level platform at the summit. Most of these pyramids have been proven to align in various ways to constellations or other astronomical measurements. And so these structures fit quite well with the concept of a "watchtower."

As a separate confirmation as to the shape of the original Tower of Babel, many scholars have suggested that the architectural model for the first tower of Babel was the **ziggurat**. The *American Heritage Dictionary* defines ziggurat as a specific form of a pyramid: "A temple tower of the ancient Assyrians and Babylonians, having the form of a terraced pyramid of successively receding stones."[24] Numerous examples of these towers still exist in Mesopotamia today.

The image of a ziggurat does not, unfortunately, suggest the kind of architectural purity that the pyramid does in the traditional sense. Instead, a ziggurat refers to a terraced structure consisting of a series of towers, one on top of the other, with vertical sections varying in height.

It is important, however, to understand the goal of constructing ziggurats in the minds of ancient men. The description of the ziggurat by the *International Standard Bible Encyclopaedia* brings out the architectural goal of the builders of these temples and their meaning among Babylonians and Assyrians:

> "These erections had, with the Babylonians, a special name: ziqquratu, meaning, apparently, 'peak,' or the highest point of a mountain..."[25]

The purpose of the ziggurat, according to this description, was to replicate the shape of a mountain and *especially the peak*! Thus, the ziggurats we are most familiar with today were intended to perform the same function as the more precisely constructed "pyramid."

"The Ziggurat of Nabonidus Restored"

We know, given the evidence in ancient Egypt, that ancient man succeeded in building incredible pyramids. Man had great organization and skills, as well as technical knowledge to build on a massive scale, even after the disruption that took place at Babel. So why not at Babel itself? Perhaps the first Tower was so thoroughly leveled that it no longer exists. This would have served as a *prophetic sign* of the severity of the destruction of the kingdom of Babel in the last days, as an indication of the absolute destruction of the "mighty mountain" as suggested by Zechariah. Hence, there are simply no traces of this Tower left today.

The image of a pyramid is certainly suggested by the prophets when they refer to Babel in the last days as a mighty, destroying mountain. This global kingdom of the last days is described as a mountain because it is a reflection of the original Tower of Babel, another "mighty mountain." It is also suggested that mankind at the first Babel was attempting to recreate the throne of God, perhaps to "reflect the heavens." As such, he used a stolen design from the very throne of God in heaven, on the utmost heights of the sacred mountain.

Finally, ever since the days of Babylon and ancient Egypt, the powerful elite of mankind have used the *pyramid* as a representation of their ambitions of worldwide unification and control. It is the quintessential building project, representing dominion over both the physical and the spiritual kingdoms of man. It is the altar on which they intend to one day establish a throne, and exalt one of their own as messiah and God (as witnessed by the capstone on the pyramid on the Great Seal). All the stones underneath the capstone fall under the control and domination of that one man, the false messiah at the summit.

For our next confirmation, we turn to the prophet Daniel.

Confirmation #5
The Rock that Falls from Heaven
During the time of the Babylonian Captivity, at some point during the seventy years of exile, King Nebuchadnezzar had a mysterious and disturbing dream.

The king summoned magicians, enchanters, sorcerers, and astrologers, and demanded that they not only interpret the dream, but that they also recall the exact events in the dream. With no information from which to work, and without the resources of God in heaven, they failed. The king then sentenced them to execution, and along with them the wise men of Israel in exile, including Daniel and his colleagues.

Faced with pending destruction, Daniel turned to God and sought the Lord for wisdom in this matter. As a result, he received a revelation through a vision, as to the nature and the meaning of the king's dream. As with Zechariah, Daniel's resulting revelation sets the stage for the entire prophetic future of mankind. The prophet Daniel begins…

Dan 2:29-30

"As you were lying there, O king, your mind turned to things to come, and the revealer of mysteries showed you what is going to happen."

Daniel then proceeds to describe the dream perfectly, to the amazement of the troubled king. The dream was a prophecy, regarding things far in the future, and it focused on a statue of man. The statue had a head of gold, chest and arms of silver, stomach and thighs of bronze, legs of iron, and feet of iron mixed with clay. This statue of a man, we are told by Daniel, was actually a series of earthly kingdoms as if on a timeline. The first kingdom was the golden head, representing Nebuchadnezzar and Babylon in the 6th century B.C. It is no coincidence that the head of the statue, Babylon ruled by Nebuchadnezzar, was the area of land in which the first Tower of Babel would have stood. The final kingdom was represented by the iron and clay feet, and corresponds to the end-time kingdom of Babel on earth. This is the kingdom referred to as the second Tower of Babel, or "spiritual Babel." As Daniel proceeds,

Dan 2:34-35

"While you were watching, **a rock** was cut out, but not by human hands. It **struck the statue on its feet** of iron and clay and smashed them."

A rock appears and strikes the statue at its feet of iron and clay. According to the timeline, the feet represent the last kingdom of spiritual Babel on earth, the unification of the world under the man of lawlessness, the antichrist. The smashing of the iron and the clay is the smashing of man's rebellious power on earth during the last days, and in a greater sense, represents the judgment of the entire system of Babel throughout the ages (note that at that point the *entire* statue comes crashing down).

In this context, we see that the statue in Daniel is the same as the mighty mountain in Zechariah. The mighty, destroying mountain and the statue represent a single underlying image: **the counterfeit kingdom to the kingdom of God on earth**.

What happens next is a fascinating revelation, and a confirmation of the presence of two mountains in Zechariah.

Dan 2:35
But the rock that struck the statue **became a huge mountain** and filled the whole earth.

As this vision from Daniel unfolds, one mountain (or statue) is destroyed and a second mountain appears. And the second mountain is not a simple mound, but an enormous, astonishing mountain whose presence fills the whole earth. And this revelation from Daniel aligns perfectly with what we saw in Zechariah: the capstone (**ro'sh**) suggested the presence of a second mountain!

Z4:7   "What are you, O **mighty mountain**? Before Zerubbabel you will become level ground." Then he will bring out the **capstone** [*ro'sh*] to shouts of 'God bless it! God bless it!'"

One kingdom falls, and another rises.

Zechariah has told us that at the time of the leveling of the mighty mountain, representative of the kingdom of Babel, a capstone will appear. And the shape of this stone implies its function; it is to cap a mountain, a mountain greater than the one destroyed. And this victorious mountain in Zechariah is the same as the "huge mountain" in Daniel, a mountain that will be so magnificent, so "huge," that its presence will fill the whole earth.

As a further indication that these are parallel accounts, note that the rock in Daniel was created not by human hands, but presumably the creative hand of God (the Holy Spirit). This echoes Zechariah 4:6, "Not by might, nor by power, but by the Holy Spirit." Furthermore, we are told that the rock is carved out from a mountain, presumably the sacred mountain in heaven where the Messiah reigns, until His return at the end of the age.

Dan 2:45

"This is the meaning of the vision of the **rock cut out of a mountain**, but not by human hands..."

That is, the Son leaves His Father's mountain in heaven (He is "cut out") in order to create a similar mountain and throne on earth. Regarding the kingdom that emerges in the shape of a mountain, we are told by Daniel:

Dan 2:44

"In the time of those kings, the God of heaven will set up a **kingdom that will never be destroyed**, nor will it be left to another people. It will crush all those kingdoms and bring them to an end, but it will itself **endure forever**."

This huge mountain is symbolic of the Messiah's kingdom, which will never be destroyed, and which will "endure forever." The rock that destroys the satanic kingdom on earth will be the crown of this victorious kingdom, and will reign as King of the world. This mountain will be Zerub-Babel's finished temple, and the sign of God's completed will manifested on earth, as in heaven. This will be the beginning of the millennial reign of Jesus Christ.

There is no specific information provided as to the shape

of the rock in Daniel, this heavenly stone that smashes the earthly kingdoms of Babel. However, it is clear that the timing of the appearance of Daniel's rock aligns with the timing of the appearance of the capstone in Zechariah. Both happen at the time of the destruction of spiritual Babel. Therefore, Daniel's huge mountain is related to the mountain beneath Zechariah's capstone, and Daniel's "rock" is related to Zechariah's "capstone." Both references combine into a single prophecy: the hands of Zerub-Babel will complete a temple in the shape of a huge mountain of stones.

Through the parallel nature of Daniel and Zechariah we can conclude that **Daniel's rock is Jesus in His princely form of the exalted Capstone!** And, we can conclude that the temple being created by Jesus Christ is in the shape of Daniel's "huge mountain."

The giant, meteor-like stone will fall from heaven and crush the statue's feet, at the time of the last stage of Babel on earth, and this will be the Messiah at His second coming. Following this victorious appearance, the rock grows into a large mountain.

What type of stone can become a large mountain?

The implication is that the spiritual mountain is an extension, or a larger version, of the rock. And this is a visual clue to its shape. *A capstone (or pyramidion) that grows in size would become a larger version of itself.* It would eventually grow to become a massive mountain of stone in the shape of a large pyramid!

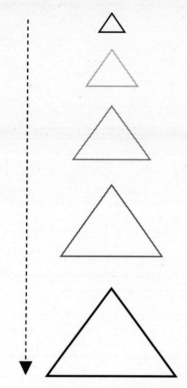

The Rock Grows Into A Huge Mountain

8

THE RIDDLE OF KANAPH
Confirmation #6

One of the very last references to Jesus Christ in the Old Testament occurs in the book of Malachi. God lays out His case against the nation of Israel, and accuses its priests of neglect and dishonesty in the priestly duties. By the end of the book, however, God shows His heart for mercy and compassion, and presents a prophecy of the coming Messiah. Like Zechariah, the prophet Malachi blends the first and second coming of the Messiah as part of a single action.

Mal 4:1-2
"Surely **the day is coming**; it will burn like a furnace. All the arrogant and every evildoer will be stubble, and that day that is coming will set them on fire," says the LORD Almighty. "Not a root or a branch will be left to them. But for you who revere my name, **the sun of righteousness will rise with healing in its wings**."

We learn of a day that is coming when the evil which plagues the earth will become like "stubble," and the descendants of evil cut off forever. But for those who revere the name of God and His Son, this day will represent the fulfillment of hope. The "sun of righteousness" will rise over mankind, and there will be an abundance of healing throughout the earth. This will be a remarkable time, when healing literally flows from the throne of God to man through the sun-like presence of the Messiah, enthroned over all.

Malachi, like Zechariah, is presenting the first and second coming of the Messiah as a single action. Healing, for instance, was certainly a major theme in Jesus' ministry at His first coming, and demonstrated the love of both the Son and the Father for man (John 6:38: "For I have come down from heaven not to do My will but to do the will of Him who sent Me"). A review of His earthly ministry, as found in the Gospels, reveals that Jesus did not refuse healing to anyone; all who came to Him were healed, and of all manners of disease.

Matt 4:23
Jesus went throughout Galilee, teaching in their synagogues, preaching the good news of the kingdom, and **healing every disease** and **sickness** among the people.

This work of healing was begun two thousand years ago, just as Zerub-Babel laid the foundation stone of His temple two thousand years ago. Since then, healing and miracles continue on earth, through the power and might of the Holy Spirit, and will only increase as we enter the last days. Malachi states, however, that there is a time coming when all disease and all sickness will be destroyed, and when disease is removed entirely from man. This will correspond with the destruction of the mighty mountain, and the presentation of the finishing stone by Zerub-Babel for His temple, at the Lord's second coming. As the beginning of the passage in Malachi suggests, this final great victory will occur at the onset of a *new day*, in which the sun-like appearance of the Messiah will rise to His earthly throne.

The Ark of the Covenant
The word used for "wings" in Malachi's passage has a special relevance for the Old Covenant tabernacle and

temple, and more specifically for the earthly throne of God. The Hebrew word used by Malachi is **kanaph**, which is connected with "overspreading" or "outstretched" wings. We have come across this idea of overspread wings before, in the furnishings of the Temple in Jerusalem, in the Holiest of Holies. Specifically, we have read that the wings of golden Cherubim covered the Ark of the Covenant, and that they were *spread across* the top, known as the Mercy Seat.

We learn more about the Ark of the Covenant in Exodus, when Moses receives instructions by God for its construction.

Ex 25:8-12
"Have them make a **chest of acacia wood**—two and a half cubits long, a cubit and a half wide, and a cubit and a half high. Overlay it with pure gold, both inside and out, and make a gold molding around it."

As for the covering of the Ark, an "atonement cover" was to be forged of pure gold, with cherubim of hammered gold at each end lengthwise. They were to face each other, and have their wings spread in such a way as to *overshadow* the cover and the Ark. The area beneath their wings was the Mercy Seat, the earthly throne of God Most High.

Ex 25:17-22
"Make an **atonement cover** of pure gold—two and a half cubits long and a cubit and a half wide. And make **two cherubim out of hammered gold** at the ends of the cover. Make one cherub on one end and the second cherub on the other; make the cherubim of one piece with the cover, at the two ends. The cherubim are to have their **wings** [*kanaph*] spread upward, **overshadowing the cover with them**. The cherubim are to face each other, looking toward the cover...There, above the cover between the two cherubim that are over the ark of the Testimony, **I will meet with you and give you all my commands for the Israelites**."

The Lord expresses the importance of the Ark of the Covenant when He says "I will meet with you [on the Ark] and give you all my commands." This Ark was to be the place of communion between God and His chosen people. In fact, the Mercy Seat was the *throne of God* on earth, the seat of His mercy and counsel.

2 Sam 6:2

...the name of the LORD Almighty, who is **enthroned** **between the cherubim that are on the ark.**

The Lord promised to appear on His throne and meet with the nation of Israel in person, and the nation was represented at this meeting by one man, the High Priest. This direct, one-on-one meeting with God was to occur in the innermost room of the temple, and upon the Mercy Seat of the Ark of the Covenant, the throne of God, under *the shadow of the wings* of the Cherubim.

David echoes this theme in the Psalms. To him, the protection and provision of the Lord were represented by the gentle overspreading of heavenly wings. David's prayers for refuge form a major theme throughout the Psalms. In the thirty-sixth Psalm, for instance, David flees for cover beneath the shadow of the Lord's wings. This was the true meaning of **kanaph** to him, fleeing to a place of refuge and protection. And it is followed with the image of men hiding under the shadow of the wings of the Lord.

Ps 36:7

How priceless is your unfailing love! Both high and low among men find **refuge in the shadow of your wings** [*kanaph*].

Other similar references to refuge under the wings of the Lord include:

Ps 57:1

Have mercy on me, O God, have mercy on me, for in you my soul takes refuge. I will take **refuge in the shadow of your wings** [*kanaph*] until the disaster has passed.

Ps 17:8-9
Keep me as the apple of your eye; hide me in the
shadow of your wings [*kanaph*], from the wicked
who assail me, from my mortal enemies who
surround me.

Furthermore, we learn that there was a specific place to
which David refers when looking for this protection. That
is, he had a visual tool in the physical realm to describe the
shelter and the refuge he found from the Lord in the spiritual
realm. We learn where this physical place of refuge resided
in the 61st Psalm. As you may have guessed, it was in the
Tabernacle (tent) of the Lord, in the Holiest of the Holies.

Ps 61:4
I long to dwell in your **tent** forever and take
refuge in the shelter of your wings [*kanaph*].

David was repeatedly referring to the image of the
overspreading wings of the Cherubim on the Ark when he
spoke of the refuge and protection of the Lord. The spiritual
truth behind **kanaph** is represented by a specific physical
location on earth, the Holiest of Holies. To be exact, it is found
under the Cherubim's wings, on the Mercy Seat of the Ark,
the throne of God.

It was there, on the Mercy Seat and in the presence of
God, that the nation of Israel found provision for its sins,
through the atoning, sacrificial blood of the Old Covenant.
The High Priest sprinkled the blood of an animal on the
Mercy Seat, reaffirming the covenant between God and man,
and the sins of the nation would be forgiven.

It was also under the shadow of these wings that Israel
found protection from their enemies, and from those who
fought against them. The Lord's favor was manifested when
Israel went to war, for wherever the ark went, the Israelites
had great victory!

The prophet Malachi introduces us to **kanaph** and
connects the image to the Messiah at His second coming.
And David connects the image of **kanaph**, the

"overspreading wings," to the wings of the Cherubim over the Ark of the Covenant, God's throne on earth.

So wherein lies the riddle?

The Riddle of Kanaph

Closer study of the word **kanaph** reveals a fascinating, yet intriguing riddle. The complete Hebrew definition includes both "overspreading wings" and a section of a building; in fact, a specific stone in a building.

kanaph

an edge or extremity; specifically (of a bird or army) a wing, (of a garment or bed-clothing) a flap, (of the earth) a quarter, **(of a building) a pinnacle**[26]

When applied to a building or temple, the word **kanaph** is the *pinnacle*!

As a refresher, the *American Heritage Dictionary* defines pinnacle as "a tall, pointed formation, such as a mountain peak," and "the highest point; summit; acme."[(18)] Just as a mountain has its peak, so a mountain of stone, the pyramid, has its peak...the capstone.

With the evidence so far, the discovery of the image of a pinnacle (or capstone) is too much of a coincidence to be overlooked. But the question arises as to how a pinnacle stone can be related, if it is at all, to the Ark of the Covenant.

The marriage of the two objects, the pyramid capstone and the Ark of the Covenant, would confirm that the throne of God is the same as the capstone, and that the pyramid was a part of God's intentional design for His kingdom.

As well, because the heavenly realm is mirrored on earth, this would hold true for both the throne of God on earth *and* the throne of God in heaven. And yet, how could a pinnacle stone possibly relate to overspreading wings and the Ark? The word **kanaph** has presented us with a riddle.

Through a series of miraculous events, the answer to this question appeared during the writing of this book. The solution, however, dated back to the early 1980s, and lay in a well-hidden place, secreted away from the world for over twenty-five hundred years. While reviewing the work of an amateur archeologist, the key to unlock the riddle of **kanaph** appeared, and in doing so confirmed the precise nature and shape of the capstone in Scripture. I was about to find out how one Hebrew word could represent two very different things: overspreading wings *and* the pyramidal capstone of the Lord's temple.

Ron Wyatt:
Our Raider of the Lost Ark

Ron Wyatt was an amateur archeologist from Tennessee who set out to solve some of the greatest mysteries of the Old and New Testaments. In doing so, he and a small team of researchers discovered numerous Biblically significant sites.

Ron proved for many that incredible things happen in people's lives when the human spirit is yielded to the Holy Spirit. A partial list of his researched sites, excavations, and new finds include:

- Noah's Ark, in the mountains of Ararat
- Egyptian grain pits built by Joseph, at Saqqara
- The Red Sea crossing, with golden chariot wheels at the bottom of the Red Sea
- Sodom & Gomorrah, with yellow brimstone balls embedded in cities of ash
- The Rock of Horeb, with signs of water erosion at the base of a giant rock
- Mount Sinai, with a blackened mountain peak "like glass," twelve pillars at the base, and an altar with petroglyphs of a golden calf

Ron Wyatt's research notes provide ample background and detail to his conclusions. The reader may easily verify these findings through the research papers and actual videos of his discoveries. His findings have been catalogued and are on display at the Wyatt Museum in Cornersville, Tennessee, south of Nashville. They are also available through the Wyatt Museum website: *www.wyattmuseum.com*.

Ron was gifted with knowledge from the Lord. One day, while walking through an area of Jerusalem known as the Calvary Escarpment, the Spirit of the Lord imparted specific knowledge to him regarding the Ark of the Covenant. Looking at a particular site, he said, "That's Jeremiah's Grotto and the Ark of the Covenant is in there."[27]

The name of this grotto is significant. Jeremiah was a prophet before and during the Babylonian Captivity. During this pre-exile state, the articles from the First Temple were removed and hidden, presumably by Jeremiah and the priests. It is also during this time that we last hear mention of the Ark of the Covenant in the Bible. Following the Babylonian captivity, which reached a crucial stage in 586 B.C., no further mention of the Ark is made in the Old Testament, and the sacred object is scarcely referred to in the New Testament. Jeremiah, therefore, was the most likely candidate to have hidden the Ark.

As support for this thesis, Ron found two non-Biblical sources, *2 Maccabees* and the *Parilipomena of Jeremiah*. Both stated that the sacred objects from the temple were hidden by Jeremiah before the destruction of Jerusalem by the invading king, Nebuchadnezzar.[28]

Ron gained permission from a senior member of the Israeli Department of Antiquities to begin excavation at this spot, which is beneath the mount where Jesus was crucified. He made slow but gradual progress in his tunnel system over the ensuing years. Eventually, he managed to dig his way into a chamber.

It was in this chamber that Ron found the articles of the First Temple. The following items are included in the list of objects he reported finding: the Table of Shewbread, the Golden Altar of Incense, the Golden Censer, the seven-branched Candlestick holder with bowl-like golden oil lamps, an Ephod, and a Miter with an ivory pomegranate on the tip. Most importantly, he found the Ark of the Covenant, sealed inside a stone case. These treasures were still wrapped in skins, buried under boards, and piled on top with rocks. Although it is not exactly clear why Ron was unable to retrieve these objects, there are two likely answers.

First, there is an earthly reason. The tunnel system was scarcely large enough for a man to fit through and was precarious. From the videos of his excavation it appears obvious that removing the large, heavy objects of the First Temple would be impossible for the time being.

Second, there was a spiritual reason. While it was most likely the right time to *find the Temple artifacts*, it was not the right time to release them to the world and the international spotlight. God has His own sense of timing, in line with His prophetic word. Biblical prophecy suggests that these artifacts will be a key feature in the very last days, when the Temple is rebuilt in Jerusalem.

Finding the Ark is incredible in itself. Mankind, and especially the elite of Babel, has searched intently for this sacred object for thousands of years. It is exciting that one man, operating through the power and might of the Holy Spirit, would accomplish in a moment what men had attempted to do for millennia. God's plan was for the Mercy Seat and the Ark of the Covenant to be in the hands of the rightful owners. The Ark is intended to be for the people of the first covenant, the nation of Israel, and for no one else.

Unfortunately Ron passed away in 1999. His work on the Ark is carefully guarded by the Israeli government and its Department of Antiquities.

What Ron did manage to provide was a reproduction of what he saw in that chamber, a drawing and subsequent painting of the Ark of the Covenant. He made the point in his research notes that this is an *exact* reproduction of what he found in that chamber. This image, published in his notes and on the museum's website, is not what the world expected to see.

A surprising aspect of the drawing is that the Cherubim are *standing beside* the Ark as opposed to *kneeling on it*. This is a significant point of variation, because the portrayals of the Ark to date have presented the Cherubim as much smaller, and in fact kneeling on the lid.

Instead, these guardian angels stand tall at attention, on either side of the Mercy Seat. Their wings are spread over the entire length of the Ark. This perspective creates a much larger Mercy Seat than previously imagined.

What causes the greatest amazement is the visual effect of the angels' wings over the ark. Ron Wyatt provided the missing link in the *riddle* of **kanaph**. The effect of the outstretched wings is this:

The wings of the cherubim form a *pyramid capstone*!

The Ark of the Covenant
with the Pinnacle Stone as the Throne of God

This drawing of what Ron saw in the chamber provides the link between the throne of God on earth atop the Mercy Seat and the image of the pyramid capstone. This is the "stone" that was described by Zechariah, the Psalmist, Daniel, Peter, Paul and others: the *capstone*, the *cornerstone*, and the *chief cornerstone*. It had been present in the Holiest of Holies, beginning with the construction of the Ark in the time of Moses. The Ark, as we know from Exodus, was built under the careful design and instructions of God. The image formed under the wings of the Cherubim was **God's**

specified design for His throne, and prophetically, **for the coming throne of His Son on earth**.

True to form, the Ark itself was placed at the highest point on the Temple Mount in Jerusalem. The Ark was thus placed *at the summit*, as the crowning stone on Mount Zion! And so the image beneath the wings was the figurative capstone at the summit of the Temple Mount; it was the "peak." As the throne in heaven caps the sacred mountain of God, so the earthly throne, the Ark, capped God's mountain on earth, Mount Zion.

And the fact that the throne on earth is in the shape of a pyramid capstone supports the theory that the central point in heaven is a mountain, also with a crowning stone as the throne at the summit. The Ark of the Covenant, like the rest of Jerusalem's Mount Zion, was a type or reflection of the much grander sacred mountain in heaven, and its utmost heights.

Throughout the priestly system of the old Covenant, when the High Priest stood before the Ark of the Covenant and atoned for the sins of an entire nation, he was facing the image of the Messiah, the Living Stone that was to come. When the high priest met with God in the Holiest of Holies, the glory and presence of God radiated from the center of the throne, shaped to fit into the image of the capstone beneath the wings of the Cherubim. There, God counseled man through the power and might of His Holy Spirit.

Kanaph in the New Covenant

We have noted before that the return of the Savior to the earth in the last days corresponds to the moment of completion of the temple of Zerub-Babel. Zechariah has told us that at this precise moment both the mighty mountain of spiritual Babel will be destroyed, and a second mountain will appear. This second mountain will be capped by the Capstone, the same stone that appeared on the Ark of the Covenant, in the protective wings of hammered gold.

For the world today, **kanaph** is just as real as it was for King David. It still designates a place of shelter, refuge, and healing. It resides over the House of God, although not the physical temple of the Old Covenant, but the spiritual temple of the New Covenant. It represents the very real power of the Holy Spirit and His rightful place as our comforter, protector and shield; the omnipresent Spirit of the living God.

Instead of the wings of the Cherubim, we find the wings of the Holy Spirit, providing an even greater source of refuge than David found in the Holiest of Holies. These wings provide shelter and they refresh our souls, like a cooling breeze in the midst of the fires of life's tribulation. God's children, reborn Gentile and Jew alike, now fall under the shelter and **kanaph** of His Spirit.

No longer is it the privilege of just one man to enter His presence in the Holiest of Holies. All those born of the Spirit may walk boldly into the presence of God, and find personal refuge in the shadow of His Spirit's wings. This is the new principle of **kanaph** for the people of God today.

Heb 4:16
Let us therefore come **boldly** unto the **throne of grace,** that we may **obtain mercy,** and **find grace to help in time of need.** (KJV)

There is great spiritual power in this concept. Making the decision to seek the shelter of the Holy Spirit is equivalent to choosing to have victory over those who seek to do evil against you. Furthermore, seeking refuge in the shelter of the Spirit's wings provides a quiet place of peace while the Lord deals with the storms of life raging outside. We are assured that when we make this decision to trust in Him and His protection and power, destruction will pass us by.

Ps 57:1
I will take refuge in the shadow of your wings [*kanaph*] **until the disaster has passed.**

A time is coming when the Ark of the Covenant will never again be sought after or held in esteem. We learn this in the third chapter of Jeremiah.

Jer 3:15-17

"In those days, when your numbers have increased greatly in the land," declares the LORD, "men will no longer say, 'The ark of the covenant of the LORD.' **It will never enter their minds or be remembered; it will not be missed**, nor will another one be made. At that time they will call Jerusalem **The Throne of the LORD**, and all nations will gather in Jerusalem to honor the name of the LORD."

A time is coming when Jesus the Messiah will return, and establish His throne in Jerusalem. This will usher in the Millennial Reign of the King over the whole of the earth. It will be the moment of completion for the temple of Zerub-Babel, evidenced by the appearance of the Capstone to shouts of celebration. It will be the return of the Living Stone, the Chief Cornerstone of all mankind. And man will loose interest in the first Ark, because Jesus will be present as the true Ark, the true testimony of God's power and might, and the new throne of God on earth. He will be the living proof of **kanaph,** as the **living Stone**.

From the original Hebrew altars in stone, to the Ark of the Covenant, to the cross of our Savior's death, and to His new covenant Temple, the Church, there has always been the capstone "waiting in the wings."

And there has always been healing in those wings.

9

THE LIGHT OF THE WORLD
Confirmation #7

Jesus is the light of the world. All forms of spiritual enlightenment outside of Him are, in reality, false light. Scripture tells us, in vivid language, that when men choose to walk by the light of another god, or even in the light of their own righteousness, they are in the dark. And when man walks in the dark, he stumbles.

Hos 14:9
The ways of the LORD are right; the righteous walk in them, but the rebellious **stumble** in them.

Malachi describes the ascension of the exalted Messiah to the throne as the image of the sun rising over the world. At the end of this age, the sun of righteousness will arise at the beginning of a new prophetic day.

Mal 4:2
"But for you who revere my name, **the sun of righteousness will rise with healing in its wings** [*kanaph*]."

We are told specifically by Isaiah that the sun and moon will be "ashamed" before the glory of the Lord, emphasizing the sun-like appearance that will be revealed on Mount Zion.

Isa 24:23
The moon will be abashed, the sun ashamed; for
the LORD Almighty will reign on Mount Zion
and in Jerusalem, and before its elders,
gloriously.

It appears that a time is coming when the spiritual light of Jesus will become the physical light of the world. The Messiah will shine forth from His throne during His millennial rule, in the same sense that God "shone forth" from atop the Ark on Mount Zion during the Old Covenant.

By virtue of the meaning of **kanaph** in Malachi's passage, we have a direct link between the Messiah at His second coming and the image of the capstone encased in the wings over the Ark. Furthermore, Malachi implies that there is a direct link between the "capstone" and the "sun of righteousness." There appears to be a deep relationship between the Messiah as the Capstone and the Messiah as the Sun, the source of spiritual light, and soon to be the source of physical light, for the world.

The image of Jesus as the sun is echoed numerous times in Scripture. For instance, Jesus described Himself as the "light of the world," and proclaimed that men walk by the light of His presence.

John 8:12
When Jesus spoke again to the people, he said,
"I am the light of the world. Whoever follows
me **will never walk in darkness**, but will have
the light of life."

Another reference to the sun-like appearance of the Messiah occurred when He was joined by Moses and Elijah on the Mount of Transfiguration. Jesus was transformed in the presence of the three disciples with Him, and He shone like the sun. Interestingly, and by design, this transfiguration occurred at the summit of a "high mountain."

Matt 17:1-2
After six days Jesus took with him Peter, James
and John the brother of James, and led them up
a high mountain by themselves. There he was
transfigured before them. His face **shone like the
sun**, and his clothes became **as white as the light**.

We learn that the Messiah will be the source of light in
the future City of God, the heavenly Jerusalem, after His
millennial rule on earth.

Rev 21:23-24
The city **does not need the sun** or the moon to
shine on it, for the glory of God gives it light,
and **the Lamb is its lamp**.

This is the same city mentioned previously, that was in
the shape of a *mountain great and high*, and which is referred
to as "the Bride." This mountain was described as being "as
high as it is long and wide," implying pyramidal dimensions,
with the Lamb as the lamp, or source of light, at the summit.

The prophetic rising of the "sun of righteousness" in
Malachi aligns with the exact moment of the ascension of
the finishing stone in the temple of Zerub-Babel, and the
moment of shouts of joy and victory in Zechariah's core
passage. Both the sun of righteousness and the capstone
appear at the dawn of a new day for mankind, a day when
the instruments of war are destroyed, when men are united
in a single purpose of service to the King, and when sickness
and disease are removed from earth. **The Stone and the Sun
both represent the coronation ceremony of Jesus Christ as
King.**

The fact that both the Capstone and the Sun of
Righteousness rise to their elevated place in the sky at the
same moment, at the onset of the Messiah's millennial reign,
leads us to the conclusion that:

**the *Sun of Righteousness* and the *Capstone* are
one and the same.**

At its arrival to the throne high above the earth, the Stone will shine like the noon-day sun. This will be the combined spiritual light and physical light of Jesus, who is repeatedly referred to as "the light of the world." *And this is why pyramid capstones are often bathed in light,* as depicted by the counterfeit and occult world of spiritual Babel.

The Glory of the Lord

For further information on the light or "glory" of God, we turn again to Scripture where we find examples of the visual manifestations of God. For instance, glory surrounded Moses as he met with God on Mount Sinai. The appearance of the Almighty, we are told, was like a cloud, and light shone like fire from this cloud.

Ex 24:15, 17
When Moses went up on the mountain, **the cloud covered it**, and the glory of the LORD settled on Mount Sinai...To the Israelites **the glory of the LORD looked like a consuming fire** on top of the mountain.

The top of the mountain looked as if it were on fire, perhaps as a prophetic image of the top of Zerub-Babel's mountain temple in the last days. And this is the same glory that entered the Tabernacle and the Holiest of Holies.

Ex 40:34
Then the **cloud** covered the Tent of Meeting, and the **glory** of the LORD filled the tabernacle.

The cloud of glory and light that represented the presence of God rested specifically on the Ark of the Covenant. When the Ark was not present, as when it was captured by the Philistines, the glory of the Lord departed Israel.

1 Sam 4:21-22
"The **glory has departed** from Israel, for **the ark
of God has been captured**."

With this in mind, we can now enter boldly into the
Holiest of Holies and witness the unraveling of a divine
secret.

An Elite Secret

The world of spiritual Babel is full of secrets, stolen from
the kingdom of God. The *core* of all their secrets is what
follows:

**The capstone on the pyramid of the Great Seal of the
United States, bathed in light and adorned with the all-
seeing eye, is the stolen image of what originally appeared
within the wings on the Ark of the Covenant!**

This is truly an amazing discovery. The image that shines
from the top of the pyramid of the Great Seal is the counterfeit
image of what appeared at the center of the true throne of
God, in the throne room known as the Holiest of Holies. The
capstone on the Great Seal is the distorted image of the
"stone" that appeared over the Mercy Seat.

The pieces to prove this have already been assembled:

I.   Zechariah informs us that the Stone that represents
     the Messiah has seven eyes.

Zech 3:9
"See, the stone I have set in front of Joshua! There
are **seven eyes on that one stone**..."

II. The Psalmist suggests that the One enthroned between
     the Cherubim shines forth from the midst of the wings.

Ps 80:1
...you who sit **enthroned between the cherubim,** *shine forth*

In this verse we learn that God is enthroned on the Mercy Seat *and* that He shines forth, like the sun, from this throne.

III. The rendition of the Ark of the Covenant in the preceding chapter displays the empty shape within the wings of the Cherubim. This empty space forms an image of the pinnacle or pyramid capstone. This is where the glory of the Lord would have manifested during His meetings with the High Priest during the Old Covenant, and His presence would have filled the space within the wings on His throne with His *cloud-like, fiery glory*.

This is why there is a capstone on the Great Seal of the United States, and why it is bathed in rays of light. The Great Seal projects the image of the counterfeit messiah spreading his false spiritual light in the same manner that God displayed His true light in the Holiest of Holies, and in the same manner that Jesus Christ will display His true spiritual light at the end of the age as the Messiah. It is a depiction of the kind of glory that appeared on God's throne on earth, stolen for the purposes of an elite corps of men. Their attempt, as at the first Tower of Babel, is to build a throne on earth to rival that of God and His Son, to "mirror the heavens." The top stone on the pyramid of the Great Seal symbolically represents this goal of *man enthroning man as God*.

After the defeat of the mighty mountain of Babel, Jesus will instead be elevated to the highest place in His pyramidal temple as the "capstone that shines like the sun." This stone will rise to the summit of the spiritual mountain of God on earth, the counterpart to the sacred mountain in heaven, and He will reign as the Sun of Righteousness.

Comparison of the True Throne of God with the Counterfeit Throne of Babel

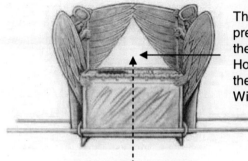

The fiery, cloud-like presence of God, with the seven eyes of the Holy Spirit, formed into the shape within the Wings

The Throne of God:
The Ark of the Covenant

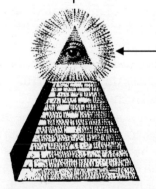

The Stolen Image of the throne that resided atop the Mercy Seat on the Ark of the Covenant

The Stolen Throne of God:
The Capstone on the Great Seal

We are informed that this Capstone has seven eyes (Zech 3:8). Likewise, in Revelation, Jesus is envisioned by John as a Lamb with seven eyes. These seven eyes are the seven aspects of the Spirit of God, the Holy Spirit (Rev. 5:6). Combining these aspects of God's presence into one picture, we arrive at the cloud-like, fiery appearance of the Lord's glory, shaped like the image within the wings of the Cherubim on the Ark, with the seven eyes of His Spirit looking out at the hearts of man. And this is similar to what is found enthroned over the counterfeit temple of Babel, on the Great Seal of the United States.

By contrast, the false light that reigns high above Satan's kingdom is, in reality, absolute darkness. The capstone and the pyramid on the Great Seal are the earthly reflections of the spiritual temple of Lucifer. And the image of the false messiah, his agent on earth, could therefore be referred to as the *"sun of unrighteousness,"* otherwise referred to by Daniel as the *"son of perdition."*

The meaning behind the capstone, bathed in light and adorned with the all-seeing eye, is a carefully guarded secret. It is a symbol that repeatedly appears in the liturgy of the elite core of spiritual Babel, as demonstrated on the Great Seal. Clearly an association has been made by the "high priests of Babel" between it and the deeper things of God. **Use of this symbol by Babel today implies that the elite of men continue to claim possession of the actual throne of God, along with its authority and power.**

As such, the representation of God in the form of a capstone bathed in light has, for the most part, been obtained through theft by Lucifer, who has transformed this image of God into an idol for worship. Therefore, the renderings of it are suspect, and more than likely *corrupted*. We are warned against worshipping graven images of any kind, including those which in some way reflect heaven (Ex. 20:4).

This is, as mentioned in Chapter Seven, a completely new image of the Messiah, Jesus Christ, for the modern Church. It is an image of God that has been dormant for over 2500 years! Ironically, the majority of followers of the secret mysteries of Babel do not know where the symbol of the capstone is derived, or that there is a link between the all-seeing capstone bathed in light and the Ark of the Covenant. But we do, thanks to this revelation from the Holy Spirit!

An Amazing Confirmation

We now know, from the Hebrew terminology set before us, and from the discoveries of Ron Wyatt, how this stone with eyes and rays of light is directly linked to the Ark of the Covenant. However, even prior to the discovery of the Ark by Ron Wyatt in the 1980s, groups of metaphysical scholars related this image to the Ark of the Covenant.

During the period between 1909 and 1911, a Swedish engineer teamed with a group of Englishmen on an expedition to the Holy Land. His name was Johan Millén, and the team was known as the Parker Expedition. They spent months digging beneath the Temple Mount in Jerusalem in search of a great archeological prize. Their published purpose, at which they succeeded, was to identify the Spring of Gihon.

Their entire mission, however, was carefully guarded in secrecy. The true intent of their efforts did not reach the public until 1917, when Millén's book, På Rätta Vägar, was released. This title, in Swedish, is borrowed from Psalm 23, which translates as "The Paths of Righteousness." In this book, Millén revealed the real reason for his team's expedition to the Holy Land. They were in search of the *Ark of the Covenant!*[29]

What is so amazing about this report, and what provides the powerful confirmation of the link between the Ark and the capstone of light with the all-seeing eye, is the cover of his book. Johan presents his "quest for the Ark of the Covenant" as depicted in the cover image that follows:

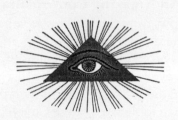

På rätta vägar

Davids forntida stad
upptäckt

Israels tio stammar
återfunna
(Äro icke judarna)

JOHAN MILLÉN

In The Paths of Righteousness
by Johan Millen

The cover displays a capstone bathed in light, with an all-seeing eye! Clearly, Millén knew that this image was of a vastly important spiritual nature, and that it was in some way connected to the Ark of the Covenant. **The very symbol defined his quest!**

From whence this knowledge came remains a secret, like much of the Parker Expedition. However, it is fair to say that at least certain Israelites would have known the nature of their God, and the image above the Mercy Seat from within the Holiest of Holies. This would have been passed down to future generations as a carefully guarded secret, and someone on this expedition apparently knew of it.

With regard to the Parker Expedition, and others like it, it is abundantly clear that what explorers, archaeologists, and even kings have been unable to do through thousands of years of research and exploration, one man did through the power and the might of the Holy Spirit. Hats off to Ron Wyatt, our "Raider of the Lost Ark."

10

THE IMAGE AT THE CENTER
(Other Confirmations)

The evidence so far has identified Jesus Christ, the true Messiah, as the pyramidal Capstone of the temple of Zerub-Babel. In the process of exploring this revelation, the evidence has also stated that the capstone is the same as the chief cornerstone, and the chief cornerstone is often referred to in a less complete form as simply the "cornerstone." All of these terms – capstone, cornerstone, and chief cornerstone – are linked through the original Hebrew and Greek terminology, which have pointed with remarkable consistency to both **a stone** and **the peak of a mountain**. The images of a stone and a mountain peak merge into a single image of the capstone, crowning a pyramidal mountain of stones, with the topmost stone representing the throne of God.

And this revelation is in agreement with the role of Jesus Christ at His second coming, which will be:

Eph 1:10
...to bring all things in heaven and on earth together under **one head**, even Christ.

This knowledge of the return of the Messiah leads us to ask whether other images of Jesus Christ are linked in some way to the pyramid capstone. That is, if this revelation is of central importance for the end-time Church, and is at the very center of the Messiah's work at His second coming, then **all other images of the Messiah should be related directly to the core image and concept of that stone.** The *image* is the capstone at the summit of the mountain of God, and the *concept* is that all creation will fall under the headship (or headstone) of Jesus Christ.

By examining other references to the Messiah, we find that the numerous other images of Jesus Christ specifically relate to this one stone.

The Righteous Shepherd

As an example of the link between the capstone and the character of the Messiah, we turn first to the image of the Lord as our Shepherd. In Scripture, God the Father, Yahweh, is compared to a "shepherd" and His followers are referred to as His "flock." We learn in a famous Psalm that the Lord God is a shepherd to His people, and in this role He satisfies all their needs.

Ps 23:1
The LORD is my **shepherd**; I shall not want.

Likewise, Isaiah presents a picture of the love of the Father for His people by applying the image of the shepherd and his flock.

Isa 40:11
He tends his flock like a shepherd: He gathers the lambs in his arms and carries them close to his heart; he gently leads those that have young.

This image applies to the Father. It also applies to the Son. The Messiah was to take on the role of the Father and demonstrate the Father's will for His people, in person. Jesus became the righteous Shepherd, and He continues even today to lead and guide His flock. The prophet Micah informs us that He does so in the majesty of the name of *His* Lord and God (that is, the Father).

Mic 5:4

He will stand and **shepherd his flock** in the strength of the LORD, **in the majesty of the name of the LORD** *his* **God**.

Similarly, the author of Hebrews bestows on Jesus the title of "that great Shepherd of the sheep." (Heb. 13:20). And Peter, the source of major revelation for the capstone, refers to Jesus as the *Chief Shepherd*.

1 Peter 5:3-4

And when the **Chief Shepherd** appears, you will receive the crown of glory that will never fade away.

There is a similarity in the two titles, *Chief Cornerstone* and *Chief Shepherd*. This is not by coincidence. In fact, Scripture affirms this connection in a number of places. With the knowledge regarding the shape of the wings on the Ark of the Covenant, we can easily make the connection between the Shepherd of Israel and the Capstone on the throne of God.

Ps 80:1

Hear us, O **Shepherd of Israel**, you who lead Joseph like a flock; you **who sit enthroned between the cherubim**, shine forth

The Psalmist has just joined the "Shepherd of Israel" with the One who sits "enthroned between the cherubim," on the Mercy Seat of the Ark! That is, *the Shepherd is the Capstone.*

These titles are applied to Jesus again in the Book of Revelation, where the Lamb is both at the center of the throne, and is the shepherd of God's people. Just as the image of the Capstone was *at the center* of the earthly throne, the Ark, so now Jesus is *at the center* of the heavenly throne, and has become a shepherd.

Rev 7:17

For the Lamb **at the center of the throne** will be **their shepherd**...

The message is uplifting. The Shepherd symbolically gathers His sheep to Him, providing both shelter and protection for His flock. So, too, the Capstone gathers its stones beneath it – the living stones – and provides shelter, protection and even refuge for them. This Shepherd is Jesus as the Living Stone, and He is the head(stone) of His Church. The stones beneath Him are, according to Peter, living stones in the kingdom of God, and they are also His flock. Furthermore, the Shepherd will be reunited with His flock at the time of His second coming, and so the Capstone will be reunited with His temple of living stones at the same time!

We find one more connection between the Shepherd and the Capstone, this time in the words of Zechariah. We are told that the Lord Himself will care for His flock, here described as the house of Judah, and He will equip them for battle against the forces of Babel in the last days. Immediately following this reference to the Lord as shepherd, Zechariah makes a related reference to the cornerstone. The prophet chooses the Hebrew word **pinnah** or *pinnacle* to describe this stone.

Zech 10:3-4
...for the LORD Almighty **will care for his flock**, the house of Judah, and make them like a proud horse in battle. From Judah will come the **cornerstone** [*pinnah*]...

The Lord Almighty will care for His flock. How? By sending His own Son as His earthly representative, Jesus Christ, the **pinnah** stone. He became a shepherd to His people, the "flock" of the first covenant, at the time of His earthly ministry. He will again be the Chief Shepherd of the Jewish nation as of His return. The Shepherd is prophesied by Zechariah to come from the bloodline of Judah, and this is fulfilled through Jesus Christ, the "Lion of the tribe of Judah" (Rev. 5:5).

Zechariah is relating the Shepherd to the cornerstone, the pinnacle stone that will finish the temple of Zerub-Babel in the last days. And as their Shepherd, He will be a source of refuge and strength for His flock.

The Righteous Branch

Similarly, we have seen before that the Messiah is compared to a righteous "shoot" or "branch." This image is, like that of the shepherd, related to the capstone in more than one instance. As with Zechariah above, the mention of the branch refers to the lineage that was to spring from the line of Judah, through Jesse, King David, Solomon and Zerubbabel. Zechariah informs us of the role of the Branch in his sixth chapter:

Zech 6:12-13

"Here is the man whose name is the **Branch**, and he will branch out from his place and **build the temple** of the LORD."

The Branch in this passage is a temple-builder. He is the architect of the Temple of the New Covenant, known as the holy nation of saints, or the Church. He is the Messiah, Zerub-Babel, who has laid the foundation stone for this temple at the cross, and who will return to place the crowning stone at the summit at His return (Zech 4:9).

We also see a reference to the Messiah as the Branch in Isaiah:

Isa 4:2

In that day the **Branch** of the LORD will be beautiful and glorious, and the fruit of the land will be the pride and glory of the survivors in Israel.

The appearance of the Branch is to be beautiful and glorious, and will occur when Israel has been through a great testing, as evidenced by the allusion to "survivors in Israel." This reference to tribulation draws our attention to the second coming of Jesus Christ, who will appear as the Capstone to shouts of victory and celebration (Zech 4:7).

Likewise, Isaiah elsewhere informs us that:

Isa 11:1-2

A **shoot** will come up from the stump of Jesse;

> from his roots a **Branch** will bear fruit. The *Spirit
> of the LORD* will rest on him—the Spirit of *wisdom*
> and of *understanding*, the Spirit of *counsel* and of
> *power*, the Spirit of *knowledge* and of the *fear* of
> the LORD

This particular passage suggests that the Branch has been endowed with the seven spirits of the Lord. These seven spirits have come to rest on the Branch, representing the Messiah. We learn in the Book of Revelation that these spirits are also presented as "seven eyes" before the throne of God (Rev 1:4). And they are purposefully pictured on the Lamb *after* it has been slain in Revelation 5:6. These seven eyes (or spirits) are the third member of the Trinity, the Holy Spirit.

The message from Revelation and Isaiah is that the Messiah has risen triumphantly from His willing sacrifice and is now endowed with the fullness of the Holy Spirit, as evidenced by the seven eyes. The Branch, or Lamb, has received *the promised gift of the Holy Spirit*.

Acts 2:33-34

Exalted to the right hand of God, he **has received
from the Father the promised Holy Spirit** and
has poured out what you now see and hear.

This is in line with what we are told in Zechariah, that the messianic Stone has seven eyes, specifically the eyes of the Lord.

Zech 3:9, 4:10

"See, the stone I have set in front of Joshua! There
are **seven eyes on that one stone**…(These **seven
are the eyes of the LORD**, which range
throughout the earth.)"

That the seven eyes in Revelation rest on the Lamb *after it has been slain* implies that this is an image of Jesus after His death and resurrection, and His subsequent ascension to the heavenly throne. This is the Messiah in His post resurrected, exalted state. Similarly, the seven eyes rest on a stone, which should also be representative of Jesus in His post-sacrifice, highly exalted state. According to the solution of the mystery in the preceding chapters, the highly exalted, post-resurrection form of Jesus Christ is the **pyramid capstone**.

The Branch, the Lamb, and the Capstone all have the seven spirits, or eyes, of the Holy Spirit. All three are representative of the exalted nature of Jesus Christ, who is adorned with the Holy Spirit of God the Father. He has received the rank and the authority of the supreme God, and He has earned the title "Lord of Lord and King of Kings."

There is yet another direct link in Scripture that ties the branch or shoot with the capstone. This fascinating proof occurs through the prophet Ezekiel.

Ezek 17:22-23

"I myself will take a **shoot** from the very top of a cedar and plant it; I will break off **a tender sprig** from its topmost shoots **and plant it on a high and lofty mountain**. On the mountain heights of Israel I will plant it..."

The planting of the branch or shoot on the top of a "high and lofty mountain" mirrors the placement of the capstone as the crowning stone at the summit. This "high and lofty mountain" is the mountain of Zerub-Babel, and the "shoot" is the Stone that will complete the mountainous temple with shouts of "God Bless It!" and which will allow the Messiah to rest from His temple-building efforts.

The tender sprig or shoot, referred to also as the "branch," will be transplanted to the summit of a *high and lofty mountain*. Where in Israel is there a high and lofty mountain? The answer is nowhere; only in the Himalayas, as mentioned, do we find truly high mountains. The "high and lofty mountain" here refers to a special place, the spiritual mountain-temple of Jesus Christ that is currently under construction: the new Mount (or Mountain of) Zion.

The Lamb That Was Slain

The connection between the Capstone and the Lamb has already been made. Because of the importance of the sacrificial Lamb to our salvation, it is worth mentioning in more detail. The link between the Lamb and the Capstone arises from the post-sacrifice and post-resurrection state of the Messiah, seated at the center of the throne in heaven. In this vision of heaven, the apostle John sees Jesus in the form of a "Lamb that was slain."

Rev 5:6
"Then I saw a Lamb, looking as if it had been **slain**, standing in the **center of the throne**..."

The vision of the exalted Messiah in heaven is of a slain Lamb, at the center of the throne. As the Passover Lamb, Jesus became our ultimate sin offering, and through the power of His shed blood He created the ongoing means for man to stand before His God, in the spiritual Holiest of Holies.

The Lamb in heaven is at the "center of the throne," and the Capstone on earth, on the Ark of the Covenant, is also at the center of the throne. Likewise, the Lamb has seven eyes and the Capstone in Zechariah has seven eyes. Both images represent the exalted form of the Messiah, who faithfully carried out the Father's will, bore our iniquities and sicknesses on the cross, and who now bears the Father's rank and His kingly seal.

Zech 3:9
"There are **seven eyes** on that one stone...and I will **remove the sin of this land in a single day**."

Another link between the Capstone and the Lamb, in addition to the seven eyes, is created through the condition of the stone. As the Passover sacrifice, Jesus Christ was tried and tested. As a sheep before her shearers is silent, He did not open His mouth before His tormentors (Is. 53:7). He was meant to pass through the furnace of affliction, according to the goodness of the Father's will *for us*, and He faced the crucible of rejection and death on *our behalf*. He was crushed for *our* iniquities. And as a result, the Lamb has been found both precious and worthy.

Rev 5:12
"**Worthy is the Lamb, who was slain**, to receive power and wealth and wisdom and strength and honor and glory and praise!"

The same language is applied to the stone the builders rejected. This stone was also tried and tested, and crushed as the *foundation stone*. Then, following this great sacrifice, the stone becomes the living, resurrected Stone and is found at the highest place in the temple, as the pinnacle or capstone. The Stone has become worthy and precious.

Isa 28:16
"See, I lay a stone [*foundation stone*] in Zion, a **tested** stone, a **precious** cornerstone [*pinnacle, capstone*]..."

The Stone, like the Lamb, is tried and tested and is found to be precious.

Other Images Relate to the Summit
There are other images of the Messiah that are related, through Scripture, to the summit of the mountain and therefore to the resting place of the capstone. A few of these are summarized below.

The Banner
Included in the growing list of references to the central message of the Capstone is the "banner." Traditionally, a banner is a rallying symbol, and a sign of victory in war. Isaiah makes the most use of this theme, and uses it as a signal to all the nations of the earth.

Isa 18:3
All you people of the world, you who live on
the earth, when a **banner is raised on the
mountains**, you will see it...

Likewise, the prophet also likens the banner to the
Branch, or the Root of Jesse. The Messiah will stand as a
banner for the nations. And the place where he rests His
throne, presumably at the utmost heights of the temple of
Zerub-Babel, will be "glorious."

Isa 11:10
In that day the **Root of Jesse** will stand as a
banner for the peoples; the nations will rally to
him, and **his place of rest will be glorious.**

Finally, we are told in Song of Songs that "His banner
over us is love." (SOS 2:4). This is a sign of the Messiah's
love for us, a love that provides shelter and refuge under the
shade of the banner, which is the stone at the summit.

Precious Metal
Through the fire of affliction, Jesus has emerged
victorious. He faced the horror of the death on the cross,
and the beatings just prior, without straying from the course
of His Father's will. This is the Stone that has been tried and
tested through the "furnace of affliction." Because He took
on our grief and sorrows, and our impurities at the cross, He
became the foundation stone that was trampled and buried.
As of His resurrection, He became like the purest of all gold
and silver. He now shines forth like the golden sun from the
utmost heights of the sacred mountain in heaven.
For our sake, God the Father said to His Son:

Isa 48:10
See, **I have refined you**, though not as silver; I
have tested you in **the furnace of affliction**.

Jesus now invites us to receive His gold, the gift so
precious that it cannot be determined by price. He invites us

to share in the riches of His eternal life.

Rev 3:18
"I counsel you to buy from me **gold refined in the fire**, so you can become rich..."

Sun of Righteousness

The link between the capstone and the sun has already been made in the previous chapter. To summarize, the Messiah as the Capstone will rise to His exalted place in the sky, enthroned over the mountain of living stones, just as the Sun of Righteousness will rise to the highest place in the sky, over the entire earth. The appearance of the capstone is the same as the appearance of the sun, and this occurs at the beginning of a new day, the Millennial Reign of Jesus Christ.

Both images refer to the same thing – Jesus as Lord of Lords and King of Kings. He will have all authority and all power over His Father's creation at the time of His second coming. Every knee will bow and every tongue confess that Jesus Christ is the King.

This concept is presented vividly in Isaiah. Instead of the physical sun being the light of the world, or the moon lighting the world by night, Jesus Christ will light the world by the glory of His presence.

Isa 60:19
The sun will no more be your light by day, nor will the brightness of the moon shine on you, **for the LORD will be your everlasting light,** and **your God will be your glory**.

The world of the occult has often referred to the *house of the rising sun* as a place of transformation, a spiritual temple where man is transformed or "birthed" into a higher self, or god. Man enters this "house," which is in reality a **pyramid**, and he is changed from mortal to immortal according to the mystery rites of Babel. The rising of the human soul to the status of a god is like the transformation of the foundation stone to the capstone, bathed in divine light. The pyramid on the Great Seal, as an example, is a "house of the rising sun." This transformation of man into the divine, like the transformation of basic stone into pure gold, is also known as "alchemy" in the world of the occult.

Again, we find an idea that has been stolen from the blueprints in heaven, and taken directly from God's plan for salvation for His people. For in the *house of Jesus Christ* we find salvation and eternal life in the kingdom of God, and we find true spiritual light, the "light of the world." We are transformed from dead stones to eternal stones, the "living stones" in 1st Peter. It is no wonder that the mystery schools of Babel seized this idea, and have used it to lead men on false spiritual journeys, apart from salvation in Jesus Christ.

The culmination of both houses, the house of Babel and the house of Zerub-Babel, will occur in the last days. The first *house of the rising sun* is the same as the mighty mountain, and Zechariah has told us that it will be leveled. It has destroyed man's soul and so it, in turn, will be destroyed. The salvation represented by this house is a lie. The greater *house of the rising sun* is the same as the temple of Zerub-Babel, and this temple will be finished when the Capstone shines like the sun at the end of the age. It will be a kingdom established forever.

Matt 13:43
"Then the righteous will **shine like the sun** in
the kingdom of their Father."

Zechariah has informed us that the battle between the forces of good and evil is like the clash of two enormous mountains, a mighty mountain representing the kingdom of Satan, and the even-mightier mountain representing the kingdom of Jesus Christ on earth. It is regarding the capstone on the evil, mighty mountain that we next turn our attention, in the section ahead.

PART
III

THE
COUNTERFEIT
CAPSTONE

11

THE GUARDIAN CHERUB

The author of Hebrews informs us that all things, especially darkness and evil, have been put under the feet of Jesus as a result of His willing sacrifice for us on the cross. Hence the sickness that entered the world at the time of the first man and woman has been defeated through the death and resurrection of the true Son of God. And yet, as we look at the state of the world, there is still much pain, suffering, and grief.

Heb 2:8-9
In putting everything under him [*Jesus*], God left nothing that is not subject to him. **Yet at present we do not see everything subject to him.**

Today, we do not see the completed will of the Messiah on earth. This is because we are living between the laying of the foundation stone and the return of the Messiah as the Capstone. As such, we continue to pray that His will for the world be made complete, "on earth as it is in heaven." Along these lines, John informs us that the kingdom of this world is not the same as the kingdom of God.

1 John 5:19
We know that we are children of God, and that the **whole world is under the control of the evil one.**

What we see around us is the battle between the kingdom of light and the kingdom of darkness. Satan is the darkness that opposes the light of God, and the antithesis to the love, compassion, and healing power of Jesus. John tells us there are no gray areas where God is concerned.

1 John 1:5
God is light; **in him there is no darkness at all**.

The world, it seems, really is black and white.

Zechariah suggests that this battle is like the clash of two giant mountains. One, the mighty, destroying mountain, represents the satanic kingdom on earth, and is a tower of the evil, occult, and even sickness that are so prevalent in the world today. The other mountain represents the kingdom of God on earth, and is a righteous tower of strength.

Ps 61:3
For you have been my refuge, a **strong tower** against the foe.

This righteous mountain demonstrates the power and the authority of the Messiah to destroy the works of darkness.

1 John 3:8
For this purpose the **Son of God was manifested**, that he might **destroy the works of the devil**.

The mighty mountain will be destroyed completely, but this will not occur until the Messiah returns to complete His temple, or tower, at His second coming. This is why John concludes the Book of Revelation with the prayer "Come Lord Jesus!" Only then will the mountain of darkness tumble, and evil be removed from the earth. In the meantime, we have the privilege of witnessing the victory over the forces of darkness through the power and might of the Holy Spirit, one life, or one living stone, at a time.

The opposing kingdom of darkness is the domain of Satan, who is likened to a terrorist: the harbinger of all that steals, kills, and destroys. He is the source of death, sickness, pain, suffering and violence. He hates God and His most precious creation, man. He was the enemy of man from the earliest days, and was the catalyst behind the separation of man from his loving Creator in Eden.

Then, he used the techniques of theft and deception to steer man's heart and destiny away from God. Today, he leads men on similar spiritual journeys apart from the knowledge of Jesus Christ: away from the realization of their salvation and from the gift of eternal life. He continues, as at the beginning, to lead peoples and nations astray.

Rev 12:9
...that ancient serpent called the devil, or Satan, **who leads the whole world astray.**

Throughout Scripture, he is also referred to as a thief and a liar. Jesus designates him as a murderer and the "father of lies."

John 8:44-45
He was a **murderer** from the beginning, not holding to the truth, for there is no truth in him. When he lies, he speaks his native language, for **he is a liar** and **the father of lies.**

Like Zerub-Babel, Satan is also a temple builder. He has been constructing a pyramidal kingdom to challenge the authority of God and His right to rule. As such, Satan sits atop his own mountain of stone, as the dark version of the chief cornerstone, in direct conflict with the temple under construction by Zerub-Babel. As the pinnacle stone, he rules over the stones beneath him, stones that are not "living stones" but rather "eternally dead stones," like himself. These lives fall into submission to the stone at the top, bathed in false light and peering out with an evil, rebellious eye. Through his global construction project, Satan seeks to establish a throne that will rival the throne of God, and he will use the man of lawlessness, the antichrist, to further this work in the last days.

Satan's power over man is based in his ability to counterfeit the things of God; doing so requires divine knowledge. The question then is, where does this knowledge come from? And, more specifically, where does his knowledge regarding the throne of God originate?

Expelled from the Sacred Mountain

It may come as a shock to learn that the source of evil, sickness and death was once a model of perfection that resided in heaven. Before his fall, Satan is described as being "full of wisdom" and "perfect in beauty." He was adorned with precious stones, and his name was originally Lucifer, meaning "brightness."

Ezek 28:12-13
"'You were the **model of perfection, full of wisdom** and **perfect in beauty**. You were in Eden, the garden of God; every precious stone adorned you...'"

He was referred to as *blameless*.

Ezek 28:15
"You were **blameless** in your ways..."

He held a place of privilege and responsibility and he was found in the most holy places in heaven. Specifically, he had access to the sacred mountain of God, especially the summit, where the throne of God resides! This is the Holiest of Holies in heaven.

Ezek 28:14-15
"You were anointed as a **guardian cherub**, for so I ordained you. You were **on the holy mount of God**; you walked among the fiery stones."

The passage above from the NIV refers to him as "a guardian cherub." The King James Version further amplifies this by referring to him as the "anointed cherub that covereth." This is essentially a job description, suggesting that his purpose was to guard and cover something of great importance. Interestingly, this phrase recalls an image we saw earlier with regard to the Ark of the Covenant.

We know from Exodus, as previously discussed, that the throne of God on earth was known as the Mercy Seat, and that it resided atop the Ark of the Covenant. Overshadowing this earthly throne were two cherubim that spread their wings and covered the whole of the seat. The cherubim symbolically "covered" and "guarded" the earthly throne of God.

The above reference to Satan as a "guardian cherub" leads us to believe that his role in heaven was similar to the role of those golden cherubim over the Ark of the Covenant. The implication is that his wings, like theirs, would have been spread as a covering for the throne of God. **The difference, however, is that his wings covered the throne of God *in heaven*, on the utmost heights of the sacred mountain.** This revelation supports the assumption that the Ark of the Covenant, and more specifically the Mercy Seat, was a model of the heavenly throne of God, and that Satan stole this image for his own purposes.

The revelation found in the writings of Ezekiel and Isaiah tells us that: Lucifer was first an angel of light, a cherub that guarded the heavenly throne, who served God in the Holiest of Holies in heaven. **And his wings would have formed the same image of the throne that we found on the Ark of the Covenant, the *pyramid capstone*.** And so he served until he rebelled and became the enemy of God.

Ezek 28:15

"You were blameless in your ways from the day you were created till **wickedness** was found in you."

At the core of his flawed character was hubris, or pride. His pride created a lust for the kind of glory, honor, and worship he witnessed while standing by the throne of his Creator. Pride sprouted like a weed in his heart and led him straight into rebellion.

Ezek 28:17

"Your heart became **proud** on account of your beauty, and you corrupted your wisdom **because of your splendor**."

Isaiah informs us that the main objective of his rebellion was to exalt himself above all else in heaven and on earth. In doing so, he would have created a throne like that of God Most High. He literally wanted to *steal the throne of God*.

Isa 14:13-14

You said in your heart, "I will ascend to heaven; I will raise my throne above the stars of God; I **will sit enthroned on the mount of assembly, on the utmost heights of the sacred mountain**. I will ascend above the tops of the clouds; **I will make myself like the Most High**."

According to Ezekiel, following this discovery of wickedness, Lucifer was cast out of heaven in disgrace, and thrown to earth.

Ezek 28:16-17

"**So I drove you in disgrace** from the mount of God, and **I expelled you,** O guardian cherub…I **threw you to the earth**…"

This great fall from grace is echoed by the prophet Isaiah.

Isa 14:12

How art thou **fallen from heaven**, O Lucifer, son of the morning! how art thou cut down to the ground, which didst weaken the nations! (KJV)

This kind of access to the most sacred place in heaven suggests that Lucifer originally had an in-depth knowledge of God's secrets and the nature of His work. And this, to answer our question before, *is the source of his wisdom*. It is stolen wisdom, gained through intimate service as a guardian cherub at the throne of the God of the universe. It was stolen through pride and rebellion, and has therefore become *corrupt*. We are told throughout Scripture that corrupt wisdom is spiritually dangerous; the mere knowledge of it caused the separation of man from His Creator in the Garden. It is also inferior to the wisdom and power of God.

Prov 21:30
There is **no wisdom**, no insight, no plan **that can succeed against the LORD**.

The Principle of Counterfeit
True wisdom comes from God. Prior to his rebellion, Lucifer was full of Godly wisdom. When he became filled with pride and chose to exalt himself instead of God, he corrupted this wisdom.

Ezek 28:17
"...you **corrupted your wisdom** because of your splendor."

Both his mind and his will became corrupt. His sense of reality was distorted, to such an extent that he saw himself as a contender for the throne of his Creator. His focus was no longer the worship of his God. Instead, his focus became the worship of himself as God. Not only did his purpose change, but his bodily features changed as well. He mutated from the "guardian cherub" to the "serpent" and the "dragon."

And the kingdom over which he rules today operates on a principle known as Counterfeit. The core tenet of this principle is best understood with the realization that there are in fact *two types* of wisdom. Likewise, there are *two sources* of wisdom...

All *true wisdom* comes from God. All *corrupted wisdom* comes from Lucifer.

The power behind the Principle of Counterfeit is that it can be difficult to tell the difference between the two. The language, symbols, and images of Satan's counterfeit kingdom on earth are all very similar to those of God in heaven. This is how the kingdom of Babel likes it, messy and confused. It is also what we would expect from the one who is trying to steal the glory and worship of God, as well as His throne.

The most precise statement regarding Lucifer's standard mode of operation is found in 2nd Corinthians.

2 Cor 11:14-15
...for **Satan himself masquerades as an angel of light**. It is not surprising, then, if **his servants masquerade** as servants of righteousness.

The forces of evil can present themselves as servants of righteousness, as Satan himself portrays himself as an angel of light. This is false spiritual light because Jesus Christ is the true light of the world. However, Lucifer and his cohorts present themselves in a way so similar to the nature of the true God and His characteristics that men are greatly confused and deceived.

Paul provides a clear and concise definition of the principle of counterfeit in the passage above when he suggests that Satan "masquerades." Paul later expounds on this when he says that the devil "schemes."

Eph 6:10-11
Put on the full armor of God so that you can take your stand against the devil's **schemes**.

It is at times difficult to grasp just how complete Satan's counterfeit message and "spiritual enlightenment" have become. As Biblical prophecy tells us, the counterfeit will become harder to distinguish in the days ahead:

2 Thess 2:9
The coming of the lawless one will be in accordance with the work of Satan displayed in all kinds of **counterfeit miracles, signs and wonders**...

Or in the words of Jesus,

Matt 24:23-24
...false Christs and false prophets will appear and perform great signs and miracles **to deceive even the elect-if that were possible**.

Satan's corrupt wisdom offers salvation and eternal life without the need to acknowledge the Lordship of Jesus as the true Messiah. Satan's wisdom is a corrupt version of the true spiritual light found in Jesus and a powerful drug in the hands of unrepentant man. Men by nature choose the path of least resistance, and search for a spirituality that tells them there is salvation without the need for repentance or change, and that righteousness comes outside the atoning blood of Jesus. As a result, men choose to follow the false light of this world, and walk instead in darkness.

2 Cor 4:3-4
The god of this age has **blinded the minds of unbelievers**, so that they cannot see the light of the gospel of the glory of Christ...

However, once the veil has been pulled back on the devil's tactics, and the light of Truth shines in, we begin to realize the extent of this spiritual counterfeit, and his corrupt wisdom begins to lose its power.

The Counterfeit Morning Star
There are many examples of Satan's counterfeits in Scripture and in the world around us. A few are provided below. One example is found in the claim of a title.

Isa 14:12
How art thou fallen from heaven, O **Lucifer** [*heylel*], son of the morning! (KJV)

The King James Version translates the Hebrew word **heylel** into the name, "Lucifer." The NIV translates the word according to its astronomical meaning to the Israelites. This was the word for the morning star.

Isa 14:12
"How you have fallen from heaven, O **morning star**, son of the dawn!"

Both translations derive their meaning from the underlying image of "brightness." In this we see a demonstration of Paul's statement that Satan masquerades as an "angel of light." There is, however, another Person who rightfully holds the title of morning star, and we learn who this is in the Book of Revelation.

Rev 22:16
"I, **Jesus**, have sent my angel to give you this testimony for the churches. I am the Root and the Offspring of David, and **the bright Morning Star**."

Jesus holds the true claim to the image of the "bright morning star." This is both a title and a message that Jesus holds dear; He specifically mentions this name in His last words to the Church in the Book of Revelation. Clearly, He wants to get this message across!

The conflict underway, between the kingdom of Babel and the kingdom of Jesus Christ, occurs in part over the meaning behind this title. What is its significance?

The morning star is the first star to rise at dawn. It announces the beginning of a new day. Prophetically, the rising of the morning star is directly tied to the appearance of the Messiah at His second coming. This will be "the dawn of a new day" and the beginning of a new era, when the Messiah will rise in victory to His throne over the earth, and when the saints will rise to reign along with him. And, as such, the morning star is linked to the resurrection into eternal life at the end of the age.

Rev 2:26, 28

"To him who overcomes and does my will to the end, **I will give authority over the nations**...just as I have received authority from my Father. **I will also give him the morning star.**"

The appearance of the Morning Star at the end of the age is also the precise moment, as has been noted, that Zechariah's capstone will appear, brought out to shouts of victory and celebration. The temple of Zerub-Babel will finally be complete at the moment that both the **capstone** and the **morning star** appear.

If you have ever watched a star at dawn, you will be able to envision the morning star rising above the horizon to its place high in the bright morning sky. In the same sense, the capstone must ascend into the dawn sky when the Messiah rises to the utmost heights of His temple, Zerub-Babel's mountain of stones. Both are representative of the return of Jesus Christ. And the conclusion, therefore, is that:

The ascension of the living Stone, or Capstone, to the summit of the Lord's Temple is *the same* as the morning star rising to its place of prominence in the dawn sky. The Morning Star is the Capstone!

This resolves another mystery, five thousand years in the making. The images of the morning star and the capstone both occur at the coming of the Messiah at the end of the age, and both rise to their elevated positions at the moment of greatest victory, the dawn of a new day. Furthermore, the morning star rises to its height in the dawn sky and literally becomes the "sun of righteousness" referred to in Malachi.

Both the rising Morning Star and the rising Capstone represent the coronation ceremony of Jesus Christ, as the King of the whole earth.

It is no wonder that Lucifer proclaims that *he* is the morning star. His ultimate goal, as has been shown, is the theft of the throne of God, as symbolized by the counterfeit capstone, and now by the claiming of the title of the morning star. Through this title, he professes to be the source of resurrection into eternal life, that he will have the position of power and authority at the end of the age, and that he will be the exalted living Stone sitting on the throne of God. All of his claims are lies. Instead, he is like the pied piper, a thief who has stolen the prophecies and images of God in order to lead peoples and nations astray.

Peter refers to the dawn of a new day, and in the same sentence makes mention of the rising of the morning star.

2 Peter 1:19
And we have the word of the prophets made more certain, and you will do well to pay attention to it, as to a light shining in a dark place, until the **day dawns** and the **morning star rises** in your hearts.

The implication is that a day will dawn that will not be darkened by night, nor by Satan's evil. This is the day of the Lord's return, His second coming. The coming Messiah will defeat the forces of Babel, and along with them the spiritual forces of Lucifer and the power of his corrupt wisdom. The mighty mountain will be crushed. And then the Messiah will ascend to His throne over the earth, like the rising of the bright Morning Star, or the Capstone bathed in light. This is the day that marks the commencement of the millennial reign of Jesus, the moment of His coronation, when the light of the Lord will rise on the hearts of all men and lead them in the way of righteousness and peace. It will be the time when healing will spread its wings over all the earth.

Counterfeit Spiritual Gifts
The principle of counterfeit is based on lies and achieved through theft. Another example of this is seen, vividly, in the spiritual gifts of the world of the occult.

We learn, for instance, in Corinthians that prophecy is a

gift to the Church. We are even told to eagerly desire it (1 Cor.14:1). This gift is to be used for the strengthening, encouragement, and comfort of the saints (1 Cor.14:2). The counterfeit to prophecy found in the kingdom of Babel is *fortune telling* and *divination*.

There is wisdom in both kingdoms, and there is power in both kingdoms. However, one source of wisdom (e.g., knowledge of the future) *is righteous* in nature, because it is revealed by the Spirit of Jesus, the Holy Spirit. The other source of wisdom (e.g., knowledge of the future) *is corrupt*, and is revealed through a spirit other than the Holy Spirit. This second form of revelation requires submission to the spiritual forces of darkness, which often masquerade as angels of light.

Another example is the gift of physical healing. This gift was demonstrated numerous times by Jesus in His earthly ministry. The authority to continue this ministry was passed on to His Church. In Matthew, for instance, the followers of Jesus are told to "preach" and "heal," among other things.

Matt 10:6-8
"As you go, **preach** this message: 'The kingdom of heaven is near.' **Heal the sick**, raise the dead, cleanse those who have leprosy, drive out demons. Freely you have received, freely give."

The counterfeit to this gift of the Holy Spirit is psychic healing, from a source other than the Holy Spirit. This type of healing is seen in the multiple forms of New Age healing techniques. Healing from this source requires submission to Babel and the spiritual forces of darkness. It is particularly sinister that the forces of darkness would entice men into false spiritual light through the prospect of health, and is yet another sign of the masquerade.

We know that ultimately one source of power is greater than the other, and that Jesus can remove the curse of darkness and spiritual blindness from our midst.

1 John 4:4
...greater is he [*Holy Spirit*] that is in you, than he [*Lucifer*] that is in the world. (KJV)

Discernment

This is why, in our defense and against the confusion of the corrupt wisdom in the world, the Holy Spirit provides us with the powerful tools of discernment. We are able to judge the good fruit from the bad, and the good gifts from the counterfeit. God foresaw the trouble His servants would have with the devil's schemes, and He knows that His children must live, at least for the time being, in the midst of the confusion of the kingdom of Babel. He provided a way through the confusion.

The first step He gave to His Church is simple: stick to the Word.

2 John 7-8

Many deceivers, who **do not acknowledge Jesus Christ as coming in the flesh**, have gone out into the world. Any such person is **the deceiver** and **the antichrist**.

Any spiritual journey or spiritual enlightenment that does not represent the historical Jesus Christ as the only Savior of man's soul is contrary to the will of God. Such spiritual journeys are flawed, and outside true spiritual enlightenment. Men who teach such a salvation are deceivers. They deny the existence of the foundation stone that was laid for our sin, at the base of the temple of the Messiah. In addition, any belief that adds to the message of salvation through God's mercy and grace, and that replaces Jesus as the one and only path to the Father, is corrupted. Not only are men who teach this salvation referred to as "deceivers," we are told that they are forerunners of the antichrist himself.

Furthermore, as our relationship with the Holy Spirit grows deeper, we receive gifts that allow us to see past the deception and schemes of the counterfeit. The Holy Spirit is the Communicator of wisdom and knowledge that comes from God. There is one spiritual gift in particular that is referred to as "discernment" or "distinguishing between spirits." It is mentioned along with the other spiritual gifts in 1st Corinthians 12. All those born of the Spirit must develop the gift of discernment as a matter of necessity, for their survival in a world of corrupt wisdom and occult.

We are told to be suspicious, to test the spirits. In the words of John,

1 John 4:1
Dear friends, do not believe every spirit, but **test the spirits** to see whether they are from God, because many false prophets have gone out into the world.

The opposite of walking in the light is blindness. And this is what occurs in growing proportion when someone willingly chooses to follow the false light and corrupt wisdom of the prince of this world.

The Counterfeit Mountain of Stone

What does all this have to do with the mystery of the capstone? The principle of counterfeit explains precisely why Christianity today thinks of the symbol of the pyramid as purely an occult object of worship. The Church has seen the corrupt, counterfeit application of a symbol and has *rightly rejected it*. However, the revelation that Satan steals the images of God, and that he is intent on stealing the heavenly throne, explains how it can be that this shape originates in heaven. It also reveals why, surprisingly, the pyramid defines the shape of the Church under construction by the Messiah, Jesus Christ.

Satan, as the guardian cherub in heaven, witnessed the inner workings and secrets of the kingdom of God. **His wings formed the same image over the heavenly throne that we find on the Mercy Seat atop the Ark of the Covenant, the image of the pyramidal capstone.** Therefore, he knows that at the center of the throne of God in heaven, on the utmost heights of the sacred mountain, the image of the Capstone *shines forth*. To establish his authority and power as the false god of earth, Lucifer has stolen the very image of the throne of God that he so closely guarded in heaven.

We learn of this in the fourth chapter of Zechariah, where

we find two kingdoms represented by two mountains, or two pyramidal temples on earth. The first is ruled over by the counterfeit capstone, and this "stone" is the source of corrupt wisdom and power for the lives underneath it. The second mountain is ruled over by the tried and tested Capstone, and this living Stone is the source of Godly wisdom and much greater power for the lives underneath it. The summit of the life-destroying mountain is the distorted mirror of the mightier, life-giving mountain being established by Zerub-Babel. And both summits are peaks (**ro'sh pinnah**), or capstones representing thrones.

The battle that has been waging for the last two thousand years, which will only intensify in the last days, is a war between two giant mountains of stone representing spiritual kingdoms on earth. We know in advance the outcome: Zerub-Babel's temple will be completed, while the mountain of spiritual Babel will be destroyed forever.

Once we gain a proper understanding of the principle of counterfeit in the kingdom of Babel, we can better understand why the world is full of counterfeit mountains of stone, known as "pyramids." This building, the pyramid, has appeared at the centers of world power, throughout the history of man and amazingly *all across the globe*. A simple list demonstrates this:

· The Pyramids at Giza, Cairo, **Egypt**
· The Pyramids of the Sun & Moon at Teotihuacan, **Mexico**
· Chichen Itza on the Yucatan Peninsula, **Mexico**
· Various Mayan Pyramid Ruins - **Belize**
· Cahokia Mounds in the Midwestern **United States**
· The Pyramids of Guimar, Canary Islands, **Coastal Africa**
· Ziggurat of Nanna - Ur, located in modern day **Iraq**
· Borobudur, in the central highlands of Java, **Indonesia**
· The Great White Pyramid - Valley of Qin Lin, **China**

The reader may be surprised to learn that the largest pyramid on earth is located not in Egypt, but rather in China! The global reach of the symbol of the pyramid is truly astonishing.

Furthermore, we find the image of the pyramid today among the elite mystery schools, secret societies that have subverted and manipulated man according to their aspiration of world domination. We saw this most vividly in the proclamation of the "New World Order" beneath the pyramid on the Great Seal of the United States.

These various pyramids are all demonstrations of the *Principle of Counterfeit*. What Lucifer saw in heaven, and the secrets he heard mentioned at the throne of God, he stole and continues to use to ensnare the hearts of man.

12

FALSE CHRISTS

As more than five thousand years of mystery surrounding the capstone begin to unravel, certain universal truths have come to light. Some of these truths have the potential to revolutionize the study of Biblical prophecy. Others may cause a shift in the understanding of the monuments of ancient Egypt, and the much sought-after meaning behind the pyramids.

One such truth concerns the image of the top stone itself. We have seen that the pyramid capstone was intended to be a representation of the exalted state of the Messiah, Jesus Christ, as a reflection of the throne of His Father in heaven. By definition, any image of a capstone on earth is a graven image and, in a spiritual sense, an idol. Therefore such stones are detestable to God. This revelation can be stated as:

The capstones of pyramids represent *false christs*.

Counterfeit Capstones

Ancient man was adept at building pyramids. The purpose behind the building of these mountains of stone was to create a "world-mountain," an earthly mirror of the dwelling of the supreme deity in heaven who reigned from a similar "sacred mountain." Typically, pyramids were capped with exalted, cornered peaks, like crowns. From the growing evidence we have before us, we can infer that these elevated stones were set on high to represent the earthly son of the supreme deity in heaven.

As dictated by the principle of counterfeit, the suspicion arises that these stones represented the earthly son of a supreme god, a son who was "god in the flesh," and who was thought to be the messiah of all mankind. The single, pinnacle stone at the summit was symbolic of an earthly throne, and a sign that the rank and authority of the supreme father in heaven had been bestowed on his son.

As a counterfeit messiah, the son reigned on earth in the same sense that his father, the supreme being, reigned over the heavens and the afterlife. As of his ascension to the earthly seat of power as king, this man became the heavenly father's sole ambassador to the peoples of earth. By virtue of his exalted capstone, he was shown to possess authority over both the physical and the spiritual worlds of man.

Thus, the construction of a pyramid, capped with a stone, was quintessential *man enthroning man as God*, precisely what took place at the first Tower of Babel! The raising of a cornerstone was the representation of the arrival of a messiah, the coronation of the next son of God, and the source of salvation for man. As such, the crowning pinnacle was a *messiah-stone*, a symbol of a false christ.

The meaning of this earthly, mountain temple is clear when one envisions a man symbolically ruling from the highest point, as the capstone, and the peoples of the earth as the stones beneath. The stones of the mountain fall into submission, and come under the control of, the utmost stone at the top. And the lofty stronghold at the summit represented the false christ's seat of power.

The capstones were therefore graven images of a false messiah, intended for worship, and they can be classified as *idols*. They were elevated, so as to challenge the authority and right of the true God to rule. The book of Exodus proclaims that any graven image meant for worship is a sin against God. This applies to images that have "any likeness of anything that is in heaven."

Ex 20:4

Thou shalt not make unto thee any **graven image, or any likeness of any thing that is in heaven above**, or that is in the earth beneath, or that is in the water under the earth. (KJV)

The capstone, as we have found, is the symbol of the *throne of God* that resided on the utmost heights of the sacred mountain in heaven. Any capstone on earth is a likeness to this most holy seat of power and therefore is a detestable idol to God. Worship of this stone, or any stone for that matter, is strictly forbidden. Any stone, *carved by man* for the purposes of worship, is against the will of the Father.

Acts 17:29

Forasmuch then as we are the offspring of God, we ought not to think that the Godhead is like unto gold, or silver, or stone, **graven by art and man's device**. (KJV)

The false messiahs of ancient times were elevated to a place of worship in the hearts of the nations, in the same sense the capstones were physically elevated to the summit of the mountain temples of stone. These capstones were the centermost idol in the mystery schools of Babel, and were the sign or "banner" of the spirit of the antichrist, the spirit that has declared throughout history that man is a god.

Ancient Egypt has provided us with the most precise examples of these stones. The exalted cornerstones rest majestically at the summits of the numerous pyramids that follow the course of the Nile. This revelation, that capstones represent false christs, fits remarkably well in the context of the Egyptian Lord of the Dead, and in the worship of his son on earth, the Pharaoh.

The Messiahs of Ancient Egypt

While the story behind the names of Egyptian gods is complex, at the core of the religion of Ancient Egypt was the belief in a supreme god in heaven and his son who was alive on earth. **Osiris** was the chief deity of the afterlife, replacing the importance of Ra, and held the title "Lord of the Dead." His wife **Isis** was known as the Queen of Heaven, and their son **Horus** was alive and well in the body of the Pharaoh, the king of Egypt.

The living pharaoh became the incarnation of Horus, the son of god, and he was worshipped as the messiah of all mankind. When he died, he was transported to heaven to become joined with his father, Osiris, and the new pharaoh took his earthly place as the son, Horus. The story of the supreme deity and his son followed a cycle that was renewed every time one pharaoh died and another took his place. This is why there was a particular sacredness attached to the bloodline of the pharaohs, and why they are known by their familial dynasties. When one pharaoh died, his son became Horus, the next messiah of the earth.

At any given point in Egypt's history, the supreme god in heaven, Osiris, had his son, Horus, seated on an earthly throne ruling over men's destinies. And the symbol of his son's reign was the *pyramid*.

The pyramid of each pharaoh was constructed during his lifetime. This temple, or house of god, was dedicated to the pharaoh as Horus, and served as a physical guarantee that he was the actual son of god in both title and deed. That is, his pyramid was considered to be a reflection of the *heavenly throne* of his father, Osiris, the supreme deity that ruled over all.

Osiris ruled from the heavenly mountain as the *spiritual capstone*, and his son Horus ruled from the earthly mountain as the *physical capstone*. It is the same principle, albeit the counterfeit version, that is found in the Lord's prayer: "on earth as it is in heaven." It is also the same idea found in the book of Hebrews, where we learn that there is both an earthly Mount Zion and a heavenly Mount Zion.

Egypt was the most powerful nation in the world at that time, and so the throne for the son of god on earth resided there. As Egypt's power waned, over the many years of its existence, power shifted to other kingdoms that came to prominence and, to some extent, ruled the world. Many of these foreign kings, however, made ceremonial journeys to Egypt to be initiated into the mysteries of Osiris, to be crowned as messiahs. These rites were officiated by a priesthood that maintained the secretive mystery schools and the liturgy with all its inherent meaning, and the core of these rites originated at the Tower of Babel.

It is worth noting that Jesus, the true Messiah and Chief Cornerstone, also journeyed through Egypt. This was meant as a powerful message to the occult kingdom of Babel, and served notice to all mankind that the actual Son of God had arrived!

Matt 2:15
And so was fulfilled what the Lord had said through the prophet: **"Out of Egypt I called my son."**

The Stele of Amenmose
One of the key Osiris narratives, handed down to us over thousands of years, is detailed on a portion of a stone column known as the Stele of Amenmose. This record in stone dates to the Eighteenth Egyptian Dynasty (1550-1305 B.C.). As the editors of *Sacred Texts Of The World* note:

> "Here, we read a long praise of Osiris, and how he is king of the gods while his son is king of the earth. Horus' kingship is directly reflected in Egyptian institutions since every living Pharaoh is Horus. Hence, praise of Horus is also the praise of the Pharaoh, son of Osiris."[30]

Certain passages on this stele bear mentioning to emphasize this point. Regarding the supreme deity Osiris we read:

> "Hail to you, Osiris,
>   Lord of eternity, king of gods,
>   Of many names, of holy forms,
>   Of secret rites in temples!"[31]

Osiris is hailed as "Lord of eternity" and as "king of the gods." He is also lord of the secret rites in temples, and the mention of secret rites reveals much about the true nature of Osiris. These rites were the basis for initiation into the secret mysteries of Egypt, and they involved a death and resurrection ceremony, a "birthing" of man into a god. The mysteries were, in essence, packages of corrupt wisdom doled out by the hands of an elite priesthood to the ruling classes, and to men of power.

These secret rites incorporated many aspects of the occult, including witchcraft, sacred prostitution, sorcery, divination, and direct communion with spirit guides. Practices such as these are mentioned in Galatians and are referred to as sin.

Gal 5:19-20
The acts of the sinful nature are obvious: **sexual immorality**, **impurity** and **debauchery**; **idolatry** and **witchcraft**…

Ironically, because these activities are sinful, they result in the opposite of the intent; sin is what *excludes* us from the presence of God and His Son. The ancient Egyptians, it seems, chose to follow the false light of Horus, and the corrupted wisdom of his father Osiris, known scripturally as Lucifer.

Any attempt to equate Osiris with the God of the Israelites, or to suggest a prophetic link between Horus and Jesus Christ will prove false when the nature of these secret rites is considered. A strong warning is put forth in the Old Testament against the kinds of practices found in these mysteries. In doing so, Deuteronomy encapsulates much of what falls under the umbrella of pagan mystery rites…

Deut 18:9-13
Let no one be found among you who sacrifices his son or daughter in the fire, who practices <u>divination</u> or <u>sorcery</u>, <u>interprets</u> <u>omens</u>, engages in <u>witchcraft</u>, or <u>casts spells</u>, or who is a <u>medium</u> or <u>spiritist</u> or who <u>consults the dead</u>. **Anyone who does these things is detestable to the LORD**…

All of these practices are at the heart of the mystery schools of Ancient Egypt and, even earlier, Babel before it. They will also be *at the core* of the worldwide kingdom of spiritual Babel in the last days.

Returning to the text on the Stele of Amenmose, we see the extent of the authority of this false christ known as Horus. Regarding the son of Osiris, we read:

> "Welcome, Son of Osiris,
> Horus, firm-hearted, justified,
> Son of Isis, heir of Osiris!
> ...Horus was found justified,
> His father's rank was given him
> ...Sky, earth are under his command,
> Mankind is entrusted to him,
> Commoners, nobles, sunfolk."[32]

The son Horus had received the authority or "rank" of his father Osiris, and as such all heaven and earth were "under his command." He had ascended his throne while his father watched from heaven. All mankind, we are told, was "entrusted to him" including commoners, nobles, and the elite that were initiated into the mysteries, referred to as the "sunfolk."

From the solution to the mystery in the preceding chapters, and the revelation of the nature and meaning of the pinnacle stone, we can infer that it was the Pharaoh's capstone resting atop his pyramid that symbolized his father's rank as well as the entrusting of all men to his care. Of all the stones used in the pyramidal temple, this one stone was the most important and powerful of all. The messianic stone at the summit ruled over the "hearts and minds" of the millions of stones beneath. Hence, the presence of the chief, pinnacle stone established for all time that this earthly king was in fact a savior of mankind, that he ruled with the authority and power of the supreme god in heaven, and that he had control over the destines of man in this life and the next.

The Obelisk

There was, in fact, another means of delivery for this most exalted of stones. Even if the resources of manpower and technical skills needed to build pyramids were lacking, as they were at various points in Egyptian history, the pharaoh was not denied his elevated place as the son of god on earth; his capstone would still be raised in honor of his claim to divinity. How was this possible? Through the use of the **obelisk**, numerous examples of which are scattered across the funerary landscape of Egypt. At the top of the obelisk sat a miniature pyramid, the pyramidion, the capstone of a pyramid.

By virtue of its shape, this one exalted stone at the top was capable of representing the entire pyramid beneath. **The obelisk was a coded reference to the presence of a much larger spiritual temple, a world-mountain of stone.** Because of this, obelisks were a sign of the presence of a son of god on earth and of the physical and spiritual dominance of one man over many. Logic has told us before that where there is a mountain peak, there is a mountain somewhere underneath. Similarly, where there is a capstone, there is likewise a pyramid underneath.

Scriptural References

The capstone is a symbol of a false christ. This is an amazing revelation. Yet, is this confirmed anywhere in Scripture? Indeed it is! We look to the prophet Isaiah for confirmation:

Isa 19:13

The officials of Zoan have become fools, the leaders of Memphis are deceived; the **cornerstones** (*pinnah*) of her peoples have led Egypt astray.

Who, according to Isaiah, has led Egypt astray? The chief cornerstones of Egypt, the **pinnah** have. Who are these chief, pinnacle stones? They are the pharaohs who claim to be Horus, the son of god. How have they led the people of Egypt astray? By presenting themselves as false christs, by ascending to their earthly thrones atop the counterfeit mountain of stones, and by sitting in the place of worship reserved for the true Son of God, Jesus Christ. Indeed, the pharaohs had "led Egypt astray" just as Lucifer has "led the whole world astray" (Rev. 12:9).

Along the lines of Isaiah's revelation, that the **pinnah** of Egypt have led the people astray, Jeremiah informs us that no pinnacle stone will be taken from the destroying mountain of Babel for the summit of the mountain temple of God. That is, no false messiah will be allowed to share the title and glory of the true Messiah, Jesus Christ.

Jer 51:26
"No rock will be taken from you [*Babel*] for a **cornerstone** [*pinnah*]..."

This revelation of *capstones as false christs* will become critical to the understanding of the worldwide government and religion of the last days, when the man of lawlessness professes to be the Son of God on earth. He will use the symbol of the capstone when he takes charge of the physical and spiritual destinies of the nations of the earth.

And once again, man will enthrone man as God.

13

THE SYMBOLS OF PHARAOH

The evidence that pyramid capstones represent false christs suggests that the pinnacle stone was at the core of the symbolism of the Pharaohs. As we have learned, these ancient kings of Egypt were the embodiment of Horus, the counterfeit messiah of mankind. The suggestion is that their right to rule, both physically and spiritually, was evidenced by the elevation of a stone to the summit of a mountain, or, as a surrogate, the obelisk.

In addition, these false messiahs of old should somehow serve as a model for the greatest of all false messiahs, the man whose reign is yet to come. There is, as we will see, evidence in Scripture that prophetically reveals this coming "man of perdition" as a type of Horus. There should be, therefore, a great similarity between the spirituality of the Pharaohs of Egypt and the spirituality of this last false christ known as the *antichrist*.

We begin to see that the coming of the antichrist will be like the coming of the gods of Ancient Egypt and, more importantly, the earlier gods of Babel. This would certainly be in line with the prophetic suggestion in the Book of Revelation that the antichrist "once was, now is not," and yet someday "will come" again.

Rev 17:8
The inhabitants of the earth…will be astonished
when they see the beast, because **he once was,
now is not**, and **yet will come**.

The Tools of a Shepherd

To begin to understand the link between the capstone,
the Pharaoh, and the coming false messiah of the last days,
we return to the image of the shepherd in Scripture. In the
words of Peter we find Jesus Christ presented as the *Chief
Shepherd*.

1 Peter 5:4
And when the **Chief Shepherd** appears, you will
receive the crown of glory that will never fade
away.

Jesus Christ, in His role as the Chief Shepherd, will
provide for his flock and offer shelter and protection. The
purpose of a righteous Shepherd is to gather his sheep
together and to watch over them. As such, the Messiah is
referred to as the Shepherd and the Overseer of our souls.

1 Peter 2:25
…you have returned to the **Shepherd** and
Overseer of your souls.

This notion of a righteous Shepherd is a parallel concept
to a Capstone that gathers its stones underneath it to shelter
and watch over them. The Shepherd and Overseer of the
kingdom of God on earth is Jesus Christ, and He is the living
Stone at the head of His temple. His sheep are the living
stones being used in the construction of this temple; they
are lives in the eternal kingdom of God. Soon, the Shepherd
will be reunited with His flock at the time of His second
coming, just as the Capstone will be reunited with His living
stones at the time of His second coming. The Capstone will
be brought out to shouts of "God Bless It!" (Zech 4:7) and in
the same sense, His sheep will know Him (John 10:14).

The conclusion, again, is that *the Chief Shepherd* and *the Chief Cornerstone* are one and the same. This was confirmed for us in Psalm 80, where the "Shepherd of Israel" is the same as the "One who is enthroned beneath the cherubim" on the Ark of the Covenant. As we saw earlier, the image enthroned between the cherubim was the pyramid capstone.

Ps 80:1
Hear us, O **Shepherd of Israel**, you who lead Joseph like a flock; you **who sit enthroned between the cherubim**, shine forth...

With this in mind, certain symbols associated with the Pharaohs of Egypt strongly confirm the mirroring of Jesus Christ, in accordance with the principle of counterfeit. One such symbol is the *shepherd*.

Each Pharaoh as Horus, the son of Osiris, clasped the tool of a shepherd, the *shepherd's crook*, as a means of demonstrating his claim to the title "chief shepherd" and his spiritual right to rule. He clearly held this instrument dear both in life and in death. The crook frequently appears, for instance, clutched tightly by the Pharaoh on the cover of the sarcophagus of the dead king. This is displayed most notably on the burial coffin of King Tutankhamen.

The Shepherd's Crook of the Pharaoh

The purpose of this tool was to remind the world of its need for spiritual guidance, and to highlight the Pharaoh's role as its messiah. It was a confirmation, albeit the counterfeit version, of Jesus' own words reflected by Peter:

1 Peter 2:25
For you were like sheep going astray...

The messiah of Egypt was a man, and thus could appreciate the specific needs of the human race, but was also the son of god and thus "had the ear" of his heavenly father, Osiris. Pharaoh's subjects were thought of as sheep, and Pharaoh, as messiah of the world, was their *chief shepherd*. He was the overseer of man's soul, a guide not just in worldly matters but also in spiritual matters, because he had the rank of his father. With his god-like nature, the Pharaoh was believed to have held the destiny of man in his hands, in this life and in the next.

His ascent to power as the *chief shepherd* was the fulfillment of his role as the *chief cornerstone* and *overseer* of the world, as a counterfeit to the words of Peter. This is why, for instance, the capstone on the Great Seal of the United States has the "all-seeing eye." The pinnacle stone and the eye represent the Shepherd and Overseer ("Over-seer") of the world.

1 Peter 2:25
...but now you have returned to the
Shepherd and **Overseer** of your souls.

For those who obeyed the rule of law, the Pharaoh led them gently with the staff of a shepherd. But for those who resisted his control and dominion over them, the Pharaoh had an alternative, cruel instrument, an instrument of power and enforcement. This tool, which he grasped in his other hand, was referred to as the *flail* or *whip*. The obvious meaning behind the presentation of these two symbols, the crook and the flail, was the totality of his reign; that his subjects could choose to obey, or they could be forced to obey. Sheep, so it seems, did not have free will in the world of spiritual Babel. They were dominated and controlled.

The Flail of the Pharaoh

We see both aspects of the Pharaoh's nature, as Horus, in the words of the prophet Habakkuk. In Habakkuk's writings we are told of a wicked world ruler at the end of the age who "gathers" the nations to him, as with the shepherd's *crook*, while at the same time he takes peoples "captive" with the *flail*.

Hab 2:4-5
"See, he is puffed up; his desires are not upright...**he gathers to himself all the nations** and **takes captive all the peoples**."

Habakkuk is introducing a link between the Pharaoh of old, the chief shepherd of Egypt, and the coming world ruler of the last days, the antichrist.

Zechariah further develops this link. He applies the symbol of a shepherd to the wicked, world ruler in the end times. In his eleventh chapter there is mention of an *evil shepherd*, a man in great contrast to the righteous Shepherd, Jesus Christ. And this man is prophetically described as holding the tools of a shepherd.

Zech 11:15
Then the LORD said to me, "Take again **the equipment of a foolish shepherd**."

Zechariah is told to take the "equipment" of a foolish shepherd, an apparent reference to the *shepherd's crook* and *flail*. And with this introduction comes a prophetic warning about the man of lawlessness, the Horus of the last days. In contrast to the good Shepherd, this alternate shepherd is an evil and worthless guardian of the flock. Rather than caring for and nurturing his flock, this evil shepherd will devour his sheep.

Zech 11:16

"For I am going to raise up a **shepherd** over the land **who will not care for the lost**, or seek the young, or heal the injured, or feed the healthy, **but will eat the meat of the choice sheep**, tearing off their hoofs."

The coming false messiah is presented as a shepherd. There is a strong historical precedent as to why the antichrist would take up the equipment of a shepherd, and why he is referred to in Biblical prophecy as an evil, foolish guardian. He will be a spiritual descendant of the kings of Babel and Egypt, he will purport to be the messiah of all mankind, and will be the "Pharaoh of the last days." His ascent to power as the *chief shepherd* over the kingdom of Satan on earth will be the fulfillment of his role as the *chief cornerstone* and *overseer* of that kingdom. As the chief cornerstone symbolically gathers the stones of the mountain beneath it, he too will gather his stones, or flock, beneath him. He will claim to hold man's destinies in his hands, and he will not easily let go.

Likewise, Isaiah has informed us that the pinnacle cornerstones (**pinnah**) of Egypt, the false messiahs, have "led the people astray." This again suggests the image of the shepherd leading his flock.

Isa 19:13

...the **cornerstones** (*pinnah*) of her peoples **have led Egypt astray**.

How much more will the chief shepherd of Babel lead mankind astray in the last days! The shepherds of Babel are represented, symbolically, by chief, pinnacle stones. They have led people, *like sheep*, astray. All of this contrasts with the work of the true Messiah, Jesus Christ.

1 Peter 2:25
For you were like sheep going astray, but now you have returned to the **Shepherd** and **Overseer** of your souls.

The true Messiah, Jesus Christ, and the false messiah of old, Pharaoh, are represented by the symbol of the shepherd as a means of demonstrating their authority over their respective flocks. This suggests that there exists a complete, counterfeit gospel in the theology of Babel, a gospel that mirrors the true gospel of Jesus Christ and promotes Horus, the false christ. We find another example of this theology in the image of outstretched wings.

The Overspreading of Wings
A symbol snatched from the throne of the Almighty, like that of the Shepherd, is the image of overspreading wings. Previously, we saw the power of this image, which rested above the Mercy Seat on the Ark of the Covenant. The overspreading wings provided both a physical and a spiritual covering for Israel. This was presented by the Hebrew word **kanaph**, and was the place of refuge and shelter for the Israelites in their God, their Rock, and their Deliverer.

Ps 57:1
Have mercy on me, O God, have mercy on me, for in you my soul takes refuge. I will take **refuge in the shadow of your wings** (*kanaph*) until the disaster has passed.

With this image in mind, and according to the principle of counterfeit, we would not be surprised to see the symbol of "overspreading wings" applied to the pharaohs of ancient Egypt, a symbol that reveals a specific characteristic of the nature of Horus. We would also expect to find this symbol of wings connected in some way to the capstones of the Egyptian pyramids that serve to glorify these false messiahs.

The fact is that Horus, the son of Osiris, was often pictured as nothing but *outstretched wings*: not the gentle wings of the dove of the Holy Spirit, but rather the wings of the falcon, the bird of prey.

The Wings of Horus   The Sun

At the center of these outstretched wings was an image of the sun; this fiery orb was seen to be rising amidst the wings. Note the similarity of this symbol of Horus with the description of the coming of the true Messiah, Jesus Christ!

Mal 4:2
"But for you who revere my name, the **sun of righteousness will rise with healing in its wings**."

This is another demonstration of the counterfeit gospel of Babel. The image of outspread wings was commonly placed over the entrance to temples, as an indication of the covering provided by this false messiah for his people. One example of the counterfeit **kanaph** is found over the entrance to the Temple of Ramesses III.

The Wings Over The Temple Of Ramesses III at Medinet Habu

Also note the contrast suggested by Scripture: instead of the light of the true Messiah as the sun of righteousness, we find in ancient Egypt the false light of an imposter as the *sun of unrighteousness*. Instead of the wings of the dove, the bird of peace, we find the wings of the falcon, a bird of prey. We see the reality of Zechariah's condemnation of the coming evil shepherd, who will prey on the sheep of his own flock.

This Hebrew word for outstretched wings, **kanaph**, has a second meaning, alternatively translated as the "pinnacle of a building;" that is, the *pyramid capstone*. The pinnacle stone, or capstone, was the image that appeared within the wings of the cherubim, which were spread over the throne of the Mercy Seat. The coming of the Messiah was prophesized on the Ark, or throne of God, in the form of the living Stone, and appeared in the shape of the stone that will complete the mountain temple of Zerub-Babel in the last days.

According to the *principle of counterfeit*, we would expect to see outstretched wings connected in some way to the capstones of pyramids in Egypt. These capstones, as suggested, are symbols of the throne of the false messiah Horus. Yet again, we find precisely this connection! These wings appear, for instance, on the topmost stone, the capstone, of the Pyramid of Amenemhat III at Dashur, pictured below.

Capstone From the Pyramid of Amenemhat III at Dashur [33]

The connection between outstretched wings and capstones on the pyramids of Egypt is *startling*. It is an image that reflects the Mercy Seat on the Ark of the Covenant, which includes outstretched wings in combination with a pyramid capstone! It confirms that the link between heavenly wings and capstones resided in the theology of Babel. Because Amenemhat III predates Moses and the building of the Ark by some 600 years, it strongly suggests that this image of wings, capstones, and thrones originates in heaven, on the utmost heights of the sacred mountain. This would have been the image that Satan, as the guardian cherub, stole following his great fall, and which he now uses on earth to establish his own kingdom and throne.

There is more to reveal, however. Remember that the glory of God appeared within the space under the wings of the cherubim on the Ark. This divine glory was like a fiery cloud of the Lord's presence, and in this cloud were the seven eyes of the Holy Spirit. Notice that on the capstone of Amenemhat III, just beneath the wings, there are the eyes of a god! Specifically, we find the eyes of Horus looking out from *his throne* atop the pyramid. Similarly, we learned that the seven eyes of God looked out onto the nation Israel from the summit of the Temple Mount, and specifically from within the image of the capstone on the Mercy Seat of the Ark.

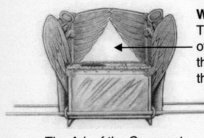

Wings, **Eyes**, and **Capstone**: The fiery, cloud-like presence of God, with the seven eyes of the Holy Spirit, appeared within the wings of the Cherubim

The Ark of the Covenant

The eyes on the capstone atop Amenemhat's pyramid are the "all-seeing" eyes of Horus. According to ancient Egyptian theology, the Pharaoh was endowed with an omnipotent, omniscient nature, along with the rank and authority of his father Osiris. His eyes, as the "over-seer" of Babel, watch over the hearts and minds of the lives below, from the stone at the summit. They are the eyes of the shepherd of Babel. Remarkably, they appear under outstretched wings and on a pyramid capstone!

Furthermore, these eyes are related to the single eye that is bathed in light atop the pyramid of the Great Seal of the United States. Both are a representation of the eyes of Horus, the false messiah of mankind.

The Eye of Horus on the Great Seal is related to the Eyes of Horus on the Pyramid Capstone of Amenemhat III.

The Pyramid & Capstone from
The Great Seal

The one set of eyes applies to the Horus of old, in this case Horus embodied by the Pharaoh Amenemhat III. The other eye, bathed in light on the Great Seal, applies to the Horus yet to come, the Pharaoh of the last days. Again, we see the fulfillment of John's words in Revelation:

Rev 17:8
The inhabitants of the earth...will be astonished when they see the beast, because **he once was, now is not**, and **yet will come**.

We will explore why Horus is presented at times with only one eye.

The appearance of outstretched wings and divine eyes on pyramid capstones in ancient Egypt confirms that the image originally chosen by God for His throne in heaven, and for His Son's throne on earth, was subsequently stolen by Lucifer. The Great Seal of the United States strongly suggests that this image has been preserved by the Mystery Schools of Babel in order to be used again, as the symbol for the throne of the false christ in the last days.

The Morning Star

The conflict over the title of the Morning Star was shown to be at the heart of the capstone mystery, and is a prime example of the principle of counterfeit. Lucifer claims this title for himself, and in Isaiah we read the contrast between his claims and reality.

Isa 14:12

"How you have fallen from heaven, **O morning star**, son of the dawn! You have been cast down to the earth, you who once laid low the nations!"

In a wonderfully ironic statement of judgment against the devil, we are told that, while Lucifer claims to be the rising morning star, he instead fell from heaven and was cast down in disgrace from the heights of the sacred mountain. This fall from such great heights is actually prophetic of his second great fall in the future, when he will be cast into the abyss at the return of Jesus Christ (Rev. 20:3).

It was also noted before that the image of the **Morning Star** and the **pyramid capstone** are *one and the same*. This was revealed through the image of Jesus at His second coming, when both the capstone bathed in light and the bright Morning Star will rise to the place of their exalted throne, over the earth. Jesus as the living Stone will return to be exalted over His temple as the crown, and His ascension to this throne will be like the rising of a star in the early morning sky. Both the Morning Star and the Capstone represent **the coronation ceremony of Jesus Christ as the King of the whole earth.**

Rev 22:16

"**I, Jesus**, have sent my angel to give you this testimony for the churches. I am the Root and the Offspring of David, and **the bright Morning Star.**"

In Isaiah 14, we learned that Lucifer claims the title of morning star for himself. It is no wonder, then, that the pharaohs of ancient Egypt also claimed the title of the Morning Star. They, like their spiritual father Lucifer, or Osiris, claimed to be in possession of the power of resurrection from the dead, and to be the spiritual light of the world at the end of the age. In line with this claim, they sat on the earthly throne set aside solely for Jesus Christ, reserved for Him since the beginning of the world. This throne was stolen to promote their claims of world dominance, and was represented by the capstone that crowned their pyramids, their counterfeit mighty mountains of stone.

The most vivid example of the application of the title Morning Star to the Pharaoh, as Horus, occurs in the Pyramid Texts from the complex at Saqqara, south of the Giza Plateau. In these texts, the title of Morning Star appears at least *seventeen times*, and is depicted mainly as a five-pointed star in its hieroglyphic form.

Heiroglyphic for Morning Star

A few of these references to the Morning Star, translated by R.O. Faulkner from the texts of Saqqara, are provided below.

Pyramid Text 1207

O Morning Star, Horus of the Netherworld, divine Falcon...Hail to you[34]

Pyramid Text 805

He sets you as the Morning Star in the middle of
the Field of Rushes, you being seated on your
throne.[35]

In the first passage, the title of Morning Star is applied
specifically to Horus, the Pharaoh. In the second passage,
we read that the Morning Star will be seated on its throne,
presumably rising at dawn to its seat of power in the sky.
This is stated even more explicitly in Pyramid Text 2014.

Pyramid Text 2012-2014

Raise yourself, O King; may you sit on your iron
throne...hands are clapped for you, feet are
stamped for you, you ascend here as a star, as
the Morning Star.[36]

Notice what takes place. The Morning Star rises to its
exalted throne while a great celebration takes place. Compare
this text to the presentation of the Capstone in our core
passage in Zechariah!

Z4:7   *"Then* he will bring out the capstone to shouts
of 'God bless it! God bless it!'"

As the capstone in Zechariah ascends to the exalted
throne of God over all the earth, great shouts of victory and
celebration occur. In the same sense, we read in the texts of
Saqqara that when the Morning Star rises to its throne,
"hands are clapped" and "feet are stamped" for the Pharaoh
as Horus. A coronation ceremony and a related celebration
are found in Zechariah and in the pyramid texts of Saqqara.
Furthermore, this is paralleled in a powerful way in Psalm
47:

Ps 47:1, 5, 8

Clap your hands, all you nations; shout to God
with cries of joy. **God has** *ascended* **amid shouts
of joy**, the LORD amid the sounding of
trumpets...God reigns over the nations; God **is
seated on his holy throne**.

God will "ascend" to His throne amid shouts of victory, trumpets, and *hand clapping*! This is the moment of the coronation of Jesus Christ as the true Messiah at the outset of His millennial rule. It is therefore the same moment as the rising of the Morning Star and the placement of the capstone on the temple of Zerub-Babel. The incredible similarity between Zechariah, Psalm 47, and the Pyramid Texts is yet another demonstration of the comprehensive nature of the counterfeit gospel of Babel. It draws us ever closer to the link between the rising Morning Star and the raised Capstone at the end of the age.

In addition, there is a surprising revelation in pyramid text 2012 above, in the reference to an **iron throne**.

The Iron Throne and the Morning Star

At the center of the pre-dynastic sun worship in Egypt was the sacred city of Heliopolis, where an obelisk known as the Innu stood. At the top of this obelisk was a capstone, the *Benben* stone, a sacred object to the early priesthood of Egypt, which maintained the mystery rites of Babel. The Benben stone was believed to have fallen from the skies, and while it subsequently disappeared from this city during the Twelfth Dynasty, its shape and nature were recorded in detail. Remarkably, this stone was in the shape of a pyramidion, perhaps by man's design. Thus, it served as a blueprint for all future capstones atop pyramids and obelisks in Egypt.[37]

In a broader sense, man has throughout time worshipped "stones that fall from heaven," or what we refer to today as meteorites. These idols are found buried beneath many of the temples of the ancient world, and legend has it that such a stone served as the foundation for the Roman Forum. It is in fact a meteoritic stone that resides in the holiest city of Islam, Mecca, behind the black veil in the shrine of Ka'ba, site of the yearly Haj. To ancient cultures, these meteorites were thought to be of sacred origin, and of the same material *as iron*. They were a type of heavenly "heavy metal" that was on occasion gifted to man.

The obvious connection here is too strong to ignore. The

king's ascension to his "iron throne" is related to the ascension of the Morning Star in PT 2012-2014. The original pyramid capstone of ancient Egypt, known as the *Benben* stone, was thought to be a meteor and as such a form of *divine iron*. It was also shaped like a pyramid capstone. As we now know, the capstone in the kingdom of God is a symbol for the throne of God in heaven, and of the throne for His Son on earth.

It appears that PT 2012-2014 refers to the ascension of the Morning Star to the iron throne atop *the pyramid*, where the Star becomes the capstone! The conclusion is that the **iron throne**, the **Morning Star**, and the **pyramid capstone** *are one and the same.*

In the world of Babel, and in the kingdom of Jesus Christ, we find a parallel between the Morning Star, the throne of the messiah, and the pyramid capstone. Accordingly, the Morning Star of the Egyptians rose to its exalted "throne" atop the pyramid, and ruled from its summit over the lives of those on earth. Because the antichrist will be the Pharaoh of the last days, and will represent Horus the false messiah, it follows that he too will claim the stolen title of his father, Lucifer or Osiris, that title being the "bright Morning Star."

The All-Seeing (False) Eye

Horus was known as the "all-seeing god," and was often pictured with a *single eye* in the shape of the sun. As an example, the overspreading wings of Horus center on the image of a sun disc, and the sun was a representation of his "divine eye."

The Sun as the Eye of Horus

This is an intriguing facet of the character of Horus, as it relates the eye of the messiah of ancient Egypt to the sun. This is especially intriguing because the capstone on the pyramid of the Great Seal of the United States is also pictured with *a single eye*. And the eye on the Great Seal emits a divine light, like the sun! It appears that the "all-seeing" eye of the Great Seal is directly related to the eye of Horus. In addition, the eye within the capstone on the Great Seal has been termed the "all-seeing eye," perfectly in line with the fact that Horus' title was the "all-seeing god." Like his father Osiris, he was the supposed source of spiritual enlightenment for man, and an omniscient force on earth.

Simply put, the "all-seeing eye" on the Great Seal's capstone is the "all-seeing eye" of Horus. Furthermore, the capstone on the Great Seal is the distorted mirror of the capstone that resided under the wings on the Ark of the Covenant; the image has been *corrupted*. The eye belongs, instead, to the false messiah Horus, the ultimate false christ.

Most intriguing of all is that there is a Biblical prophecy that suggests the coming antichrist, the Pharaoh of the last days, will have sight in just one eye! To understand the true significance of this prophecy, we return to the words of Zechariah, where we learn of the coming of an evil shepherd.

Zech 11:16

For I am going to raise up a **shepherd** over the land **who will not care for the lost**, or seek the young, or heal the injured, or feed the healthy, **but will eat the meat of the choice sheep**, tearing off their hoofs.

This evil shepherd is going to receive a wound to his head. We learn this when we see the antichrist pictured in the Book of Revelation as the head of a beast.

Rev 13:2-3

One of the heads of the beast seemed to have had a **fatal wound, but the fatal wound had been healed**.

Zechariah tells us exactly what the effects of this wound will be:

Zech 11:17
"Woe to the **worthless shepherd**, who deserts the flock! May the sword strike **his arm** and **his right eye!**"

It appears that the evil shepherd, the antichrist, will receive a wound to his head and will recover, although it will paralyze an arm and blind his right eye. The effect would be the image of the false christ, the chief shepherd and overseer of Babel, reigning as the capstone over the earth *with just one eye.* Zechariah suggests that the "all-seeing eye" of this false messiah is in reality a false or blind eye. That is, the partial physical blindness of the antichrist will be symbolic of his spiritual blindness to the true nature and character of God. Zechariah draws subtle attention to the image of the antichrist *as a type of Horus,* and as a Pharaoh of the last days.

The capstone above the pyramid on the Great Seal mysteriously speaks of this as well, with its one "all-seeing" eye. Something must explain the reason for this single eye in the annals of ancient Egyptian prophecy.

Such prophecy includes a story in which an epic battle is waged between a man and his uncle. The uncle is named Seth, and it was he who was responsible for the death of Osiris, his brother. Seth infamously scattered the pieces of his slain brother's body around the nations of the world. On his death, Osiris then became ruler of the afterlife, the supreme deity of all.

In a scene reminiscent of Shakespeare's Hamlet, the son (Horus) takes vengeance on his uncle (Seth) for the murder of his father, the king (Osiris). A battle ensues, and in the course of this battle one of the two gods loses his *right eye.* No guess necessary as to which one; it was Horus, the one-eyed, yet all-seeing, false messiah.

The words of the prophet Zechariah, the image on the Great Seal, and the prophecies of ancient Egyptian all point to the coming of the antichrist as a type of Horus, the one-eyed, false messiah of mankind.

14

In the World Around Us

The mystery rites of Osiris and Horus were recorded throughout ancient history. They appear strategically in the form of the mystery schools at the seats of world power. This was certainly the case in Egypt, and Babel before it. It was also the case in ancient Greece, and later in Rome. There appears to have been a means of preserving the nature and meaning of these rites, as if there was a society responsible for keeping the metaphysical torch burning, a grand master of all grand masters. This may not seem like such an incredible feat, until you realize the length of time between the beginnings of the ancient rite in Babel, the transfer to Heliopolis in Egypt, to the rise and fall of the Roman Empire. This represents more than three thousand years!

Horus Enters Rome, And U.S. Commerce

When Osiris, Isis, and Horus appear on the scene in Rome, their names have changed to Saturn, Diana, and Jupiter, respectively. Thus Osiris became Saturn, the supreme god over all. And Horus became Jupiter, the son of god and messiah of the earth.

Regarding Jupiter as the messiah, the Roman poet Virgil wrote his *Fourth Eclogue* in 40 B.C. In this work, Virgil presents a hope for a new age, a dawn of a new era on earth led by the savior of man. It was in this poem of messianic deliverance that Virgil introduced the phrase **"Novus Ordo Seclorum"** that now appears below the pyramid on the Great Seal of the United States.

The Great Seal of the United States

VIRGIL:
A Glorious,
New Order
Of The Ages

This phrase is translated variously as a "Glorious Age," a "New Order of the Ages," or simply a "New World Order." Specifically, Virgil was placing the hope for the renewal of mankind on a young man, the adopted son of Julius Caesar named Caius Octavian, who was later to be known as Caesar Augustus.[38] It was the young emperor Augustus who was to embody the god Jupiter when he ascended the throne over the Roman Empire, just as the pharaohs of Egypt embodied the son of Osiris, Horus. Through his coronation, Augustus was to become the messiah over all. Indeed, he was even claimed to have been of virgin birth!

In this poem, the *Fourth Eclogue*, Virgil proclaims that Saturn (Osiris) has been re-established as the supreme god, and with this divine act, justice has returned to the world. This new world order was made possible by a new type of man, who, it seems, was endowed with the authority and power of the heavenly father. Upon his arrival, a glorious age (*novus ordo seclorum*) will begin.

The new age will be led, Virgil implies, by a new race of men, presumably the elite of mankind who have been initiated into the secret rites of Babel, and who are therefore transformed into "gods." These elite men, by virtue of adoption by the supreme deity, were to become as brothers to Jupiter (Horus). This would have resulted in a worldwide brotherhood of god-like men. This is the counterfeit message to what Paul tells us in Romans and Ephesians, that all those in Christ Jesus are adopted into the family of God, and become sons of God.

This kingdom, Virgil emphasizes, will encompass both the spiritual and the physical worlds of man. For instance, this child of Saturn will remove all sin from mankind; he will free men from the fear of death (presumably through his gift of eternal life); and he will sit on his father's earthly throne ruling over men, in a world finally at peace. Sound familiar? Jupiter, or Horus, was to lead the world on a spiritual journey into a false salvation, apart from Jesus Christ.

Virgil's poem of messianic deliverance is the source of the quote below the pyramid on the Great Seal, a phrase which alludes to **a golden age to be introduced by a false messiah**. This is all the more disturbing when we realize that this poem is being applied almost two thousand years after Virgil, by the crafters of the Great Seal. This brings the mystery rites and symbols of Babel into present time, spanning a period of over five thousand years!

Virgil's description and messianic ideal have been compared by scholars to the seventh and ninth chapters of Isaiah. The references to the coming messiah of virgin birth, who will usher in a world at peace, are all too similar to the prophecies regarding Jesus Christ to ignore. As Tupper

Saussy, author of *Rulers of Evil*, notes, "Virgil borrowed heavily from the messianic verses of Isaiah, whose writings were freely accessible through the Jewish rabbis of Rome."[39] This is a potent reminder that the principle of counterfeit is fundamentally the principle of theft.

The Word of God, not to be outdone by Virgil's prophecy, answers back. Paul, writing in the years following Virgil's work, describes this current age not as *golden*, but rather as *evil*.

Gal 1:3-4

Grace and peace to you from God our Father and the Lord Jesus Christ, who gave himself for our sins **to rescue us from the present evil age**...

The men who crafted the Great Seal of the United States, at the time of the country's founding, were initiates into the mysteries of spiritual Babel. Of this there is no doubt. They wanted to make sure the future initiates of Babel did not miss the reference to the messiah in the banner beneath the pyramid. As if to provide a clue as to the meaning of the capstone on the Great Seal, and as to the authorship and meaning of "novus ordo seclorum," a second link was made to the same poet, Virgil.

The crafters of the Great Seal included a second line from this same poet, but from a different work, and this line wraps around the top of the pyramid. Above the capstone with the all-seeing eye, it is rendered "**Annuit Coeptis**." A common translation for this quote reads "God hath favored this undertaking," and this phrase appears in the Ninth Book of Virgil's *Aeneid*.[40]

Thus, there can be no doubt that it is Virgil's *Fourth Eclogue*, and the announcement of the arrival of the messiah of the world, that is being referred to on the Great Seal of the United States, as well as on the back of the dollar bill. Could there be any question, then, that the capstone bathed in light and with the "all-seeing eye" is meant to be Virgil's messiah Jupiter, the son of god in Roman times, who was originally Horus of Ancient Egypt?

ANNUIT COEPTIS:
God Hath Favored This
Undertaking (Virgil)

The Great Seal of the United States

There is one important aspect of Horus, however, that is lacking from this image on the Great Seal: *overspread wings*. For this characteristic of the ancient false messiah, we simply turn the Great Seal over, and compare the image of the Eagle on the back side (or the right side of the dollar bill) to Horus the Falcon. The following image of Horus was recovered from the burial chambers of the kings of Egypt, and bears remarkable similarity to the Eagle on the Great Seal.

First, there is an obvious likeness in the position of the outstretched wings; the wings themselves are an image of Horus. Second, notice the impressive similarity in the position of the sun burst (or sun disc) that appears directly above the heads. Third, notice that both the Eagle and the Falcon hold symbols of power in their talons, the Egyptian "ankh" in the clutches of the Falcon, and the arrows and olive branch in the clutches of the Eagle. Finally, there is a subtle, yet forceful connection being made to the Tower of Babel, as previously suggested through the image of the

Horus the Falcon, with Outstretched Wings

The Eagle on the Great Seal

pyramid on the opposite side of the Seal. This occurs in the Latin phrase on the banner in the mouth of the Eagle. It reads **"E Plurbis Unum,"** which is translated, "Out of many, One." This kind of global unification was the objective of rebellious man at the first Tower of Babel, and is, in essence, the role of the pinnacle capstone in both the kingdom of God and the kingdom of Babel.

The connection between Horus and the Great Seal may raise some concerns about the founding of the United States, as mentioned before, yet there is no suggestion that all of the founding fathers of the nation were involved in secret societies that promoted false messiahs. Rather, the Great Seal demonstrates that the forces of spiritual Babel have touched the shores of America, just as they have reached *every other nation*. The presence of these symbols on the Great Seal confirm that as a new seat of world rule is established, the rites of Osiris and Horus are quick to follow, hidden in the hallowed halls of power. Furthermore, their presence suggests that the *spiritual battle* between the forces of good and evil, as represented by the clash of two mountains in Zechariah, is being waged on a significant scale within the United States itself.

It should also be noted that there is indeed a new age coming, a *novus ordo seclorum*. This will occur when the true Messiah returns. The evil prince of this world, Lucifer, will be done away with, along with his false messiah Horus, and the mighty mountain of Babel will be destroyed. Jesus will instead sit on the throne as the true Son of God and King of the world. Those who have chosen to follow the true Messiah will be called "saints" and will receive an inheritance, eternal life. And they will become co-regents with the newly arrived King, in His power and authority and grace! They will become the true "golden race" who will rule along side Jesus.

Rev 20:6
...they will be priests of God and of Christ and will **reign with him for a thousand years**.

Obelisks Among Us

With the significance now attached to the image of the capstone, it is important to recognize that there is another means of delivering this stone to the world, a means other than the pyramid. The capstone is the stone that sits atop the obelisk, and it is just as much a symbol of the counterfeit messiah as a stone atop a pyramid.

It may be surprising to find that there are carefully selected obelisks dotting the landscape of the major capitals of the western world. They sit quietly, gathering little attention, as if waiting for the appropriate time to be revealed for what and who they really are.

One such obelisk resides in London, the capital of the United Kingdom, along the river Thames. Another stands in the Place de la Concorde in Paris, the capital city of France. There are thirteen in Rome, the most important being the obelisk that now stands in the center of St. Peter's Square. There are obelisks in the United States; one resides in Central Park in New York, the financial capital of the world, one resides in Washington D.C. This modern version, known as the Washington Monument, has a large capstone at the top and a smaller, aluminum pyramid at the very summit. **All of these capstones, according to the principle of counterfeit, represent *false christs*.**

In fact, there are so many obelisks, spread throughout the world, that combined they seem to represent a *worldwide system of false christs*, otherwise known as the spirit of the antichrist.

15

THE STONE OF LAWLESSNESS

The solution to the mystery of the capstone is being revealed today, for the Church, because it will be central to the unified purpose of Babel in the last days. We may assume that the arrival of the Pharaoh of the last days, his elevation as the son of god in the flesh, and his ascension to the throne over the unified kingdoms of man, will coincide with the veneration of the symbol of the false christ, the **pyramid** and the **capstone**.

We get a strong hint of this from Paul in Thessalonians:

2 Thess 2:2-4
He will oppose and **will exalt himself over everything that is called God or is worshiped**...

The antichrist will exalt himself over everything that is called God and over anything that is worshiped. *This is precisely the kind of spiritual domination suggested by the image of the capstone over the pyramid.* It is also an echo of Lucifer's ultimate goal before his fall, to sit on God's throne "on the utmost heights of the sacred mountain." The presentation of the capstone would be a powerful sign that the whole world is being brought under the control and supervision of one man. As the stones of the pyramid are brought into submission to the chief stone at the top, so the lives of most of men and women will be subject to the reign of the man of lawlessness enthroned on high.

In his attempt to steal the throne of God, the antichrist will claim to be the earthly representative of the supreme being, the son to the father, Horus to Osiris, the false messiah serving the counterfeit god of the world.

Accordingly, we expect there to be in the last days a return to the mystery rites of ancient Egypt and Babel. We expect the name Horus and Osiris to become known again, in some form. We also expect the antichrist to pay homage to the source of his power and authority, to worship a god who claims the image of the capstone. Are there references in Scripture, or elsewhere, regarding the nature of his god?

The mystery schools of Egypt have suggested that the rank, authority, and power of Horus were given to him by his father, Osiris, lord of the afterlife. In the same sense, we expect the future Horus to pay homage to a god that is also his father, and who is the source of his authority, rank and power.

It is interesting to find that this coming world ruler is referred to in Scripture as the "son of perdition," implying that there must be a "father of perdition," the source of all eternal damnation. When Osiris is revealed for whom he is, not the lord of the afterlife but the lord of the eternally damned, then the title "son of perdition" fits perfectly to his son, Horus.

Likewise, we find that the antichrist is the "man of lawlessness," and his father therefore would be the "god of all lawlessness," a being that has fully rejected all of God's commands and laws. This certainly reminds us of the rebellion of Lucifer and his corrupted wisdom. And we learn that the coming false messiah will lead the world into a time of great rebellion against the Most High.

2 Thess 2:3-4
...for that day will not come until the **rebellion** occurs and the man of **lawlessness** is revealed, the man doomed to destruction.

This will be a greater rebellion than that which occurred at the first Tower of Babel thousands of years prior. Spiritual rebellion leads to the rejection of God's laws and commandments, and establishes a law of its own. This is exactly what we find in Daniel. The man of lawlessness will try to change the existing laws, spiritual and otherwise.

Dan 7:25
He [*the antichrist*] will speak against the Most High and oppress his saints and try **to change the set times and the laws.**

We have also seen that the powers of rebellion are the same as, or perhaps in some way release, the powers of witchcraft. Witchcraft is defined essentially as *one person's control over others.*

1 Sam 15:23
For **rebellion** is as the sin of **witchcraft**...

Hence that topmost stone of the kingdom of darkness will greatly influence, manipulate, and control the hearts and minds of those beneath it, the lives on earth in the last days.

The God of Fortresses
With this thought, we turn to the prophet Daniel to find a fascinating reference to the god that will be worshipped by the antichrist. In the eleventh chapter of Daniel, the prophet provides a clue as to the nature of this god. This Pharaoh to come will worship a "god of fortresses."

Dan 11:36-38
He [*the antichrist*] will show no regard for the gods of his fathers...nor will he regard any god, but will exalt himself above them all. Instead of them, **he will honor a god of fortresses** [*ma'owz*]...

The Hebrew term used here for "fortresses" is **ma' owz.** Its definition includes "a fortified place, a rock, and a stronghold." Not by coincidence, all of these images are consistent with terms applied to the top of a pyramid. This deserves some exploration.

The summit of the Temple Mount in Jerusalem, where the Ark of the Covenant and the Mercy Seat (or throne) resided, was often referred to as a place of strength, as the "fortress" of God. There are two words in the Old Testament that are used interchangeably to bring out this concept: **ma'owz** and **matsuwd**. Both refer to a castle, a defense, or a stronghold. Similarly, we have shown that the throne of God in heaven resides at the top of a sacred mountain, and is guarded by the most powerful of angels, the cherubim. Whether on earth or in heaven, both summits are, according to Scripture, *fortresses* and *strongholds*.

The conclusion is that the mountain summit represents the throne of God and *the fortress that houses it*. As Ezekiel informs us in his vision of the high mountain,

Ezek 43:12
All the surrounding area on top of the mountain will be most holy.

We traced this idea back to the earliest civilizations of man, where we learned that the top of the "world-mountain" represented the throne, or dais, of the supreme deity. In some cases the summit of this mountain was simply a throne, in other cases the summit was a temple, and still in others, *it was a castle or fortress housing all of the above*. This is similar to what is found in the ruins of castles from medieval times, where the king's throne was in a fortress and the fortress was on a mountain summit. The castle served as a *fortress*, and for this reason a castle is often referred to as a *defense*. This is also why the top of a mountain can be considered to be a *stronghold*.

Moving from the physical application of this idea to the suggested symbolism of the pyramid, the capstone is analogous to the throne, and can be extended to include the entire fortress at the summit. Both in the physical nature of the fortress, and in the spiritual symbolism of the pyramid, **the summit of the mountain was the well-guarded seat of power.**

To further confirm this idea, God is equated at various

points throughout Scripture as the "rock," the "fortress," and even the "mountain fortress."

Ps 18:2
The LORD is my **rock**, my **fortress** and my **deliverer**; my God is my rock, in whom I take **refuge**.

Likewise, Isaiah alludes to the dwelling place of God when he informs us as to where the righteous may dwell.

Isa 33:15, 16
He who walks righteously and speaks what is right...this is the man who will **dwell on the heights**, whose refuge will be the **mountain fortress**.

The reference to a mountain fortress implies a residence at some considerable height. This lofty residence of God is in line with the image of the "utmost heights of the sacred mountain" in heaven. It is also a reflection of the throne of the Son of God on earth where He will one day reign.

With this background, we can understand the term used to designate the god to be worshipped by the antichrist: *fortresses.*

Dan 11:38
...he [*the antichrist*] will honor a **god of fortresses**...

This is a reference to the counterfeit god of the world, Satan, sitting on his throne atop his mountain of stones. We recall the words of Isaiah:

Isa 14:13
You [*Lucifer*] said in your heart, "I will ascend to heaven; I will raise my throne above the stars of God; **I will sit enthroned on the mount of assembly, on the utmost heights of the sacred mountain.**"

The conclusion drawn from the reference in Daniel is that the antichrist will worship a god of ages past - more specifically a god linked to the image of high mountain fortresses, symbolically a *god of capstones*. **This god will be Lucifer disguised as Osiris.**

The Chief Prince at Armageddon
(Like Father, Like Son)

So far, there have been a number of confirmations that the graven image of the capstone represents a false messiah, a counterfeit son of god on earth. In addition, we find confirmations in Scripture that the antichrist will use the symbol of the capstone to exalt *himself* on the throne of all mankind as Horus, son of Osiris. One such confirmation is found in the book of Ezekiel.

The confirmation arises out of an account of the end time battle of the true Messiah against the false messiah. This is related by the prophet Ezekiel.

Ezek 38:3-4

"This is what the Sovereign LORD says: I am against you, **O Gog, chief prince** of Meshech and Tubal."

This prophecy informs us that the worldwide leader in the last days will have a symbolic name of Gog, and he will be a chief prince. He will command a mighty army, a "great horde" that will march on Jerusalem and attack the people of God.

Ezek 38:15-16

"You will come from your place in the far north, you and many nations with you, all of them riding on horses, a **great horde**, a mighty army. You will advance against my people Israel like a cloud that covers the land."

In this contest between the forces of light and the forces of darkness, the Lord God will gather all of his enemies

THE STONE OF LAWLESSNESS   189

against the people of Israel, giving Him the opportunity to exact one final crushing blow against spiritual Babel. This great army will be the military arm of the worldwide kingdom of the antichrist, and they will advance against Israel.

The specific consequences of this battle create a prophetic link between Ezekiel's account of Gog and the battle at Armageddon found in the Book of Revelation. The battle will be spiritual Babel's final attempt to destroy God's people, just prior to the Messiah's return.

Rev 16:14-16

...they [the evil spirits of the antichrist] go out to the kings of the whole world, to gather them for the battle on the great day of God Almighty. ...Then they gathered the kings together to the place that in Hebrew is called **Armageddon**.

A few similarities in Ezekiel's account and the version in Revelation are worth noting in order to demonstrate that the two passages refer to the same epic battle.

At the time of the battle of Armageddon, the Lord will cause thunder and storms (Rev. 16:18). This also occurs at the battle of Gog and Israel (Ez. 38:22). Specifically, hailstones of a "hundred pounds each" will fall on the armies of the antichrist (Rev. 16:21), and "hailstones" will fall on the armies of Gog (Ez. 38:22).

Similarly, at the time of Armageddon, the Lord will cause a "severe earthquake" (Rev. 16:18). This quake is so powerful that no other earthquake in the history of the world compares to it. Likewise, we read of a "great earthquake" that will take place in the land of Israel, the place where the forces of Gog are gathered to attack (Ez. 38:19).

Following the thorough defeat of the forces of Babel, the birds of the air are gathered to consume the flesh of the armies, which will apparently be so enormous that it will take years to bury all the dead. This gathering of the birds is found in both Rev. 19:17 and Ez. 38:17.

Finally, there are two key phrases in Ezekiel that confirm the alignment of his prophecy with the return of the Messiah and the establishment of His millennial rule just after the battle of Armageddon. First, there is the phrase we found previously in our core passage in Zechariah, that upon the completion of the temple of Zerub-Babel, "then you will know that I am Lord."

Ezek 38:23
"Then they will know that I am the LORD."

Second, there is a specific reference to the defeat of the forces of Gog as the "day of the Lord," the same day referred to in Psalm 118, with the appearance of the capstone: "the day the Lord has made."

Ezek 39:8
This is the day I have spoken of.

Clearly Ezekiel is presenting Gog as the false messiah and ruler of the world, the antichrist with his armies at the battle of Armageddon. This occurs at the time of the great day of the Lord's return.

Having identified Gog with the forces of the antichrist at the battle of Armageddon, we find a powerful confirmation of the antichrist's link to the image of the counterfeit capstone. A fascinating revelation is found in the Hebrew words used to describe this world ruler: he is given the name "Gog" and the title "chief prince." In these terms we find a strong echo of the capstone!

Ezek 38:3-4
"...I am against you, **O Gog, chief prince** [*ro'sh*] of Meshech and Tubal."

The Hebrew word used for chief is "**ro'sh**," and we have come across this word before. This was the word used to designate the summit or peaks of mountains, as in Genesis 8:5, Numbers 14:40, and Isaiah 42:11. It was also the word that both Zechariah and the Psalmist used to describe the capstone of Zerub-Babel, the finishing stone of the mountain temple.

Zech 4:7
"Then he will bring out the **capstone** (*ro'sh*) to shouts of 'God bless it! God bless it!'"

Ps 118:22
The stone the builders rejected has become the **capstone** (*ro'sh pinnah*)...

In addition, the summit of the *original Tower of Babel* was referred to as **ro'sh**! The construction of this tower marked the first time man attempted to enthrone man as God, following the flood.

Gen 11:4
And they said, Go to, let us build us a city and a tower, whose **top** (*ro'sh*) may reach unto heaven... (KJV)

There appears to be the suggestion in Ezekiel that this world ruler will lay claim to the image of the pyramid capstone, with all its inherent meaning. This falls in line with the relationship already established between the ancient pharaohs of Egypt and the coming false messiah in Biblical prophecy, the Pharaoh of the last days.

An alternative translation of the "chief prince" in Ezekiel would be the "prince of Rosh," or more precisely, the **prince of the capstone**. That is, the antichrist will proclaim himself to be the exalted and enthroned pinnacle stone, in place of the tried and tested, righteous living Stone that is Jesus Christ. He will be the *false messiah*, and as such will be the *counterfeit chief cornerstone*.

Second of all, while the name Gog is elusive in terms of its root source, a lesser known derivation has been suggested for the name of this world leader. It is rendered "mountain" and even "high mountain."[41] If this meaning of the name Gog is applied, then an even more specific image emerges, and the whole phrase reveals an incredible title!

"The *exalted prince* of the *capstone* of the *high mountain*"

That all three concepts are joined into one title is breathtaking. The ruler to come will be a wicked prince, he will use the symbolism of the capstone, and he will reign from a high mountain summit – an earthly version of the "mighty mountain." As Zechariah told us so eloquently from the start, we are to contrast the righteous Tower of Babel (Zerub-Babel's temple) with the unrighteous Tower of Babel of the last days (spiritual Babel). One mountain is leveled, another is set in place. **Both the kingdom of Babel and the kingdom of God are presented throughout Biblical prophecy as large mountains of stone in the shape of pyramids, with the throne of a messiah at the top**.

In the first instance, spiritual Babel is the "mighty mountain:"

Zech 4:7
"What are you, O **mighty mountain**? Before Zerubbabel you will become level ground."

In the second instance, spiritual Babel is the "destroying mountain:"

Jer 51:24,25
"Before your eyes I will repay Babylon (*Babel -* בָּבֶל)...I am against you, O **destroying mountain**, you who destroy the whole earth," declares the LORD.

And now, in the passage from Ezekiel above, spiritual Babel is led by the man Gog, the "exalted capstone of the high mountain."

The three mountains presented by Zechariah, Jeremiah, and Ezekiel are actually one and the same. They represent a mountain of evil that is the kingdom of Satan and all its resident darkness on earth. Enthroned at the top of the earthly counterpart of this large mountain is the prophetic figure of the *antichrist*: the single, blasphemous, counterfeit capstone, and the **ro'sh** of the spiritual tower of Babel. This is the abode of the false messiah, the counterfeit son of god known as Horus. And the lofty stronghold at the summit represents both his throne and his claim of world domination.

His throne will be a reflection of his father's seat of power. And his father will be Lucifer masquerading as Osiris, Lord of eternally dead stones, the god of "mountain fortresses;" that is, the god of pyramid capstones.

16

THE DARK SIDE OF KANAPH

Three times now, from three separate sources, we have seen the image of the end-time kingdom of Babel in the form of a mountain. Zechariah refers to this evil presence and great foe of the kingdom of God as a "mighty mountain." Jeremiah refers to it as a "destroying mountain." And Ezekiel refers to the head of this kingdom as the "prince of the capstone of the high mountain." Could it be that all these references are suggesting something greater than anyone has yet imagined?

We explore this growing suspicion in the account of Daniel, with regard to the mysterious nature of the "abomination that causes desolation."

The Overspreading of Abominations

Logically, the next step is to take a look at the centermost event in the reign of spiritual Babel in the last days. This event is referred to as "the abomination that causes desolation." An analysis of the language used to describe this prophetic event will provide a deeper understanding of what is portrayed, and open doors for further revelation.

The exact nature of this abomination has always been a mystery to Bible translators as well as students of Biblical prophecy. The description of what takes place is couched in vague language, as if Scripture has been purposefully holding back this particular revelation until the appointed time. It is, nonetheless, a key moment in the reign of spiritual

Babel; Jesus Himself makes mention of it in his warning to the Church regarding the last days!

Matt 24:15-16

"So **when you see** standing in the holy place '**the abomination that causes desolation**,' spoken of through the prophet Daniel-let the reader understand- then let those who are in Judea flee to the mountains."

Something ominous will occur in the holy place, the center of Jerusalem. It will be *seen*, and it will be a *cause for fleeing*. Jesus specifically advises the reader to understand this event, implying the need for further analysis. In the passage above, He references the prophet Daniel, who describes this same event in the ninth and eleventh chapters.

Dan 11:31

His [*the antichrist's*] armed forces will rise up to desecrate the temple fortress and will abolish the daily sacrifice. Then they will set up the **abomination that causes desolation**.

The Hebrew word for abomination implies a "filthy, detestable idolatrous thing." This is especially harsh language considering that Scripture already takes a hard line against idolatry. That this one act receives such a strong rebuke speaks to the singular importance and severity of the event. This abomination will be an affront to the very nature of God, and will bring devastation to the earth. We learn more about this a few chapters earlier in Daniel.

Dan 9:27

And on a **wing** [of the temple] he will set up **an abomination that causes desolation**, until the end that is decreed is poured out on him.

We read that on the *wing* of the temple, he will set up the abomination. The King James Version of this passage leads us into more familiar territory:

Dan 9:27
...and for the **overspreading** of abominations
he shall make it desolate... (KJV)

We have two translations of the same word: *overspreading*
and *wings*. The implied reference to overspreading wings is
reminiscent of a crucial image we have seen before. The
spreading of wings previously appeared in the description
of the Mercy Seat, the throne of God on the Ark of the
Covenant. The underlying word in Hebrew in that case was
kanaph, which referred to the outstretched or overspread
wings of the Cherubim. Remarkably, this is the exact Hebrew
word used by Daniel with regard to the abomination of
desolation:

Dan 9:27
And on a wing [*kanaph*] ... he will set up **an
abomination that causes desolation**, until the
end that is decreed is poured out on him.

The contrast here between Godly **kanaph** and demonic
kanaph is stark. The first, as we saw earlier in David's words,
brings a sense of protection, refuge, and peace, as in "He
will cover you with his feathers, and under his wings you
will find refuge" (Ps. 91:3). The second, *dark* **kanaph** brings
a sense of desolation, devastation and destruction, evidenced
by the "the abomination that causes desolation."

With regard to the Ark of the Covenant, we have seen
that the alternative definition for **kanaph** was "pinnacle,"
as in the peak or summit of a mountain. It was the shape
created by the wings over the Mercy Seat on the Ark, the
image of the *capstone under the wings*. It was also the shape of
the stone that Zechariah said would be brought out to shouts
of "God Bless It!" and which will crown Zerub-Babel's
mountain of living stones at the Messiah's return. It was the
image of the coming Messiah and His millennial reign.

Looking back to the counterfeit messiahs of ancient
Egypt, the image of **kanaph** appeared on the capstones of
the pyramids of the pharaohs, combining the images of

outstretched wings, eyes, and pinnacle stones. Furthermore, Horus was often depicted as nothing else but outstretched wings. Here, Daniel contrasts the image of the outstretched wings on the Ark of the Covenant with the image of the outstretched wings of Horus in the world of Babel, a symbol to be adopted by the Pharaoh of the last days.

We know the shape that these wings formed over the Mercy Seat on the Ark; it was the pyramid capstone. We have since learned that the antichrist will worship a *god of capstones*, or a god of high mountain fortresses, a reference to Lucifer masquerading as Osiris. Now we find the mention of the pinnacle stone at the center of the most dramatic event in the coming world order, a mysterious act of abomination in the holiest of cities, Jerusalem!

What is gradually appearing from the fog surrounding this remarkable event, this "abomination that causes desolation," is the elevation of a physical idol with a shape related to the Ark of the Covenant, a shape specifically linked to the top of the Mercy Seat. This would be the representation of a dark version of **kanaph**, the pinnacle stone of the kingdom of Satan on earth.

The conclusion is this: the momentous event during the reign of the antichrist, the central act of his reign, will be the physical demonstration of the greatest of all spiritual idols and abominations. It will be...

the recreation of the throne of God on earth.

This harks back to the first Tower of Babel, when man in rebellion first attempted to enthrone man as God. And it recalls the reason for Lucifer's revolt in heaven:

Isa 14:13-14
You [*Lucifer*] said in your heart..."**I will sit enthroned on the mount of assembly, on the utmost heights of the sacred mountain**. I will ascend above the tops of the clouds; **I will make myself like the Most High**."

The Shape of Things to Come

Godly **kanaph** resided atop the Ark of the Covenant, and within the shape of the wings of the cherubim. God appeared in His glorious, fiery cloud and provided counsel through the seven eyes of the Holy Spirit from the center of that throne. The demonic counterfeit of **kanaph** is also a capstone bathed in light, adorned with an ever watchful, all-seeing eye, as witnessed on the Great Seal. It is representative of the earthly throne of the false messiah, and is a reflection of the spiritual throne of his father Lucifer, the counterfeit supreme deity.

This image of the counterfeit capstone was the stone that was intended to crown the first Tower of Babel, at the summit or **ro'sh**, as the key event in man's attempt to enthrone man as God. It was why the first Tower was said to "reflect" or "mirror" heaven, or to copy the very throne of God. This abomination was why God intervened and destroyed the first Tower of Babel. It appears that the capstone of Horus will again be the reason for the dramatic intervention of God on earth, and for the final destruction of Babel in the last days!

Through the warnings of the prophet Daniel, words that are later referenced by Jesus, there is yet another indication that Babel will be in the form of a mountain with a peak, a stone in the shape of a pinnacle. In Daniel's case, however, this image is no longer just symbolic. It will become a *physical reality*. We are told that it will be seen, and it will be a cause for people to flee.

Matt 24:15

"So **when you see** standing in the holy place 'the abomination that causes desolation...'"

This provides a strong implication of things to come. We can conclude that the image of the capstone, which is in fact the pinnacle (or **kanaph**) stone, will appear *on the Temple Mount in Jerusalem*, the holy place to which Jesus refers. **Just as the image of the Godly capstone appeared on the Temple Mount and suggested the presence of the *true Messiah*, so** the counterfeit capstone will also appear on the Temple Mount and will allude to the presence of the *false messiah*. This pinnacle stone will be the stolen image of the throne of God, and will be the throne from which the antichrist reigns in the last days.

This leaves the question as to how the abomination will be elevated to a worshipful height.

The Delivery Mechanism

We know from various Biblical prophecies that the Jewish nation will rebuild the Temple of Solomon and re-instigate the sacrificial system prior to the return of the Messiah. They will experience peace in their land, and as a result they will befriend this man of lawlessness who comes as a wolf in sheep's clothing. When the Jews realize that the antichrist is not their friend, that he is instead an evil shepherd, they will revolt. And when this happens, the man of perdition will begin his destruction of their holiest site; he will take over the city of Jerusalem and in particular the Temple Mount. At this point, the abomination occurs.

Just prior to the setting up of this "abomination," there is a great devastation wrought on the holy city by the invading armies of the antichrist.

Dan 9:26
The people of the ruler who will come will **destroy the city and the sanctuary**.

The Hebrew word for "destroy" in this passage from Daniel is the same word used to describe the destruction of Sodom and Gomorrah in Genesis; this word therefore implies an utter and complete devastation. Daniel suggests that the destruction that takes place to the sanctuary in Jerusalem is complete, and the temple of the Jews is leveled.

This creates a remarkable prophetic balance between the history of the holy city and its future. The first invasion of the Babylonians, those warriors from the land of "Babel," ended with the complete destruction of the Temple of Solomon in 586 BC. Daniel implies that the second great invasion of Babel, in the last days and prior to Armageddon, will also result in the destruction of the Temple of Solomon, this time the rebuilt house of God. If this is to be the case, there is no need to limit the abomination to the confines of the temple, as it will have been destroyed. Indeed, God professes in Jeremiah that He will take "vengeance for His temple" (Jer. 50:28).

It is also important to note that in Daniel 9:27 the phrase "of the temple" has been inserted into the NIV in an attempt to pinpoint the vague meaning behind this event. That phrase does not appear in the underlying Hebrew text, which is why it is bracketed in the NIV, and is why it is absent in the King James Version.

Dan 9:27
And on a wing [*of the temple*] he will set up an abomination that causes desolation...

The only other references to the location of this abominable image are provided by Jesus and Paul. Jesus informs us that the abomination will take place in the "holy place" (Matt. 24:15). This holy place could very well apply to the site of the temple, or even the Temple Mount, rather than the temple itself.

Paul states that the man of lawlessness will "set himself up in God's temple, proclaiming himself to be God" (2 Thess. 2:4). The Greek word he uses for temple is commonly used in the New Testament to describe the temple in Jerusalem during Jesus' ministry. It is, however, also the word that Paul uses in Ephesians, where he describes the spiritual house of God, the pyramidal temple with Jesus Christ as the *Chief Cornerstone*.

Eph 2:20-22
...with Christ Jesus himself as the **chief cornerstone**. In him the whole building is joined together and rises to become **a holy temple in the Lord**.

This implies that the "pinnacle of the temple" could be the summit of a pyramidal temple as described by Paul. Indeed, it would be difficult to imagine a pinnacle stone somehow capping a rebuilt, rectangular Temple of Solomon. With this in mind, a more complete understanding of Daniel 9:27 occurs when amplified definitions are used for the underlying Hebrew text:

> And **upon** or **above** (*'al*) there will be a **pinnacle** [*kanaph*] that will be an **abomination** [*shiquwtsiym*] which will cause utter **amazement, astonishment** and **desolation** [*mashomeem*].

The original rendering in the Hebrew text indicates that on a "pinnacle," perhaps the utmost heights of a temple in the shape of a mountain, an abomination will be set in place. The pinnacle, presumably in the shape of a pyramid capstone, will be the greatest abomination in the eyes of God: the theft of the image of His heavenly throne, and its establishment as the ultimate act of rebellion in His holy city Jerusalem.

The answer to the riddle behind the dark version of **kanaph**, it seems, has been reaching out to us since the words of Zechariah in his infamous core passage. It has been subtly solidifying as the specific image of spiritual Babel presented by Jeremiah, Ezekiel, and others. The more complete answer to the question of "What is the abomination that causes desolation?" is this:

The Mighty Mountain!

The image of spiritual Babel that has been lurking in the shadows of Biblical prophecy will become a reality of *grand, physical proportions.*

The Mighty Mountain

As the Temple of the Jews is destroyed, a massive building project begins for a very large pyramid in Jerusalem. The tempting logic here is that the Tower of Babel will be rebuilt, this time at the spiritual center of the world, Jerusalem, a city that has always been the holy city of God. This Tower will be the sign of the ultimate, worldwide rebellion against the Most High God, against His laws and commands, and against His right to rule on earth. This project will confirm the counterfeit messiah as the "man of lawlessness," a man who has so thoroughly rejected the law of God that he sets up the most vile of idols, the image of the stolen throne of God, on the previous site of the Ark of the Covenant.

The suggestion that the Tower of Babel will be rebuilt is brought out through Daniel in the Old Testament and Paul in the New Testament. Both inform us that the coming of the false messiah and his desolation will not happen until a great *rebellion* occurs.

Dan 8:13
...the **rebellion** that causes **desolation**...

2 Thess 2:3
Don't let anyone deceive you in any way, for that day will not come until the **rebellion** occurs and the man of lawlessness is revealed...

There has been only one other time when the world was wholly united in this magnitude of rebellion against God; this was demonstrated through the construction of the first Tower of Babel. At that time, *man attempted to enthrone man as God*, and the throne at the summit was the capstone, or **ro'sh**, high atop a man-made mountain. In the last days, the world will once again unite in rebellion, and man will similarly use a building project as a focal point for this rebellious regime. As before, this structure will allow for a man to be enthroned as God. The construction of a large pyramid *in Jerusalem*, as a reproduction of the original Tower of Babel, with the crowning *messiah stone* on top, would be a sign that their rebellion was truly against the Most High God!

We have learned that the antichrist will serve a god of pyramids and capstones (a "god of fortresses"), and it is logical to assume that he will reign as an earthly representation of such. The summit of this mountainous tower will be the throne of the world ruler, the physical representation of Gog, the "prince of the capstone of the high mountain." Horus will again reign as the false messiah, bathed in light and adorned with the all-seeing eye.

What greater fulfillment could there be to the words of Zechariah, who informed us thousands of years in advance, that Babel will be in the shape of a *mighty mountain*, and that at the time of the Lord's return, this mountain will become *level ground*?

> **Z4:7** "What are you, O mighty mountain? **Before Zerubbabel you will become level ground.**"

Spiritual Babel, described before as a mountain and pictured as such on the Great Seal of the United States, will become a physical mountain, a modern day Tower of Babel. Certainly there are enough references to this end-time kingdom as a mountain to suggest that it may be physical as well as spiritual. We can also assume that there would be a physical representation of the image Zechariah uses to describe the entire kingdom of Babel in the last days. That is, the idea that the spiritual mountain becomes a physical mountain aligns with the precise nature of Biblical prophecy, where things spiritual often become physical realities; "as above, so below," or "as in the spiritual world, so in the physical world."

Jeremiah and the Rebuilt Tower of Babel

The specific shape of Babel in the last days was introduced by Zechariah as an imposing mountain, a "mighty mountain." It was confirmed by Jeremiah who, like Zechariah, alludes to Babel as a mountain, specifically a "destroying mountain." The prophet Jeremiah actually has much to say on this subject, and his 51st chapter in particular provides an expanded version of the story unfolding in Zechariah.

Interestingly, in Jeremiah's 51ˢᵗ chapter, we find evidence to support the construction of a new Tower of Babel. The prophet also suggests that this Tower will share the same characteristics as the "abomination that causes desolation" in Daniel. The case he makes is presented below:

I. *Babel Will Reach the Skies*
There is a suggestion in Jeremiah 51 that the Tower of Babel will be recreated in the last days.

Jer 51:53
"**Even if Babylon** (*Babel* - בָּבֶל) **reaches the sky** and **fortifies her lofty stronghold**, I will send destroyers against her," declares the LORD.

Jeremiah implies that Babel will be rebuilt. He says "even if Babel reaches the skies," and "even if Babel fortifies her lofty stronghold," she will still be destroyed. This suggests that Babel will again raise a mighty tower, similar to the tower on the Plain of Shinar long ago after the flood. The top of this tower will be at a considerable height; it will "reach the sky" and will have at the summit a "lofty stronghold." This implies a very large pyramidal mountain of stones.

II. *The Lofty Stronghold*
The word Jeremiah uses for here for "lofty stronghold" has a literal meaning: an "elevated place." All the Biblical references to the capstone are consistent with the elevated, lofty platform at the summit: *lofty stronghold*...mountain fortress...a god of fortresses...the pinnacle of abominations...the counterfeit capstone!

III. *Both the Foundation Stone and the Pinnacle Stone*
Earlier in the same chapter Jeremiah informs us that neither the foundation stone nor the cornerstone (*pinnah*) will be taken from Babel in the building of the new temple of Zerub-Babel, Jesus Christ.

Jer 51:26
"No rock will be taken from you for a

cornerstone [*pinnah*], nor any stone for a **foundation** [*yoceed*], for you will be desolate forever," declares the LORD.

Neither the corrupt wisdom of Babel nor its false messiah will have any part in the kingdom of God. This verse also implies that Babel will have both kinds of stones to offer, a foundation stone and a capstone! **A "destroying mountain" that has a foundation stone and a pinnacle stone is a** *pyramid*. This again suggests that the mountain will be a physical reality as well as a spiritual one.

IV. *The Burned-Out Mountain*
The word Jeremiah uses to describe the destruction of this mountain relates back to the story of the first Tower in Genesis. In Jeremiah 51, we learn that Babel will be a "burned-out mountain."

Jer 51:25
"I will stretch out my hand against you and make you a **burned-out mountain** [*serephah*]."

The word used by Jeremiah to describe the destruction or "burning out" of the mountain (**serephah**) is used in a derivative form to describe the "firing of the bricks" in the original story of Babel in Genesis 11:3. The prophet is again drawing a connection between the destroying mountain of the last days and the original Tower of Babel. The suggestion is that the strength of the rebellion and solidity of the Tower will be of no avail when faced with the wrath of the Son of God and the blast of His fury, unleashed at His return.

V. *Zerub-Babel, the Coming Messiah*
This word for the "burning up" of the mountain also has relevance for the core passage from Zechariah, and echoes the victory of the Messiah at His return. Jesus was prophetically named **Zerub-Babel**, because "Zerub" or "Zarab" means to *burn up, to scorch*. In the prophetic words of Zechariah, the Messiah will "burn up" the mighty

mountain and the kingdom it represents. Thus, Zechariah presents the One who will "burn up" the mountain of Babel, and Jeremiah presents the aftereffect of this victory: the "burned-out" mountain! Interestingly, the word Jeremiah uses to describe the devastation of this mountain (**serephah**) specifically implies the fires of *cremation*, suggesting there will be a conflagration resulting in an ash or dust-like refuse, as a remnant of this mighty Tower. Many prophets, including Daniel, suggest the same. (More on this "dust-like refuse" in Section IV.)

VI. *Two Images, One Purpose*

There is a strong similarity between the destroying mountain and the abomination of desolation. Both Jeremiah's *mountain* and Daniel's *abomination* cause desolation. They share a similar purpose, a similar reason for being.

Jeremiah appears to be referencing the "abomination of desolation" when he suggests the destructive power of the mountain of Babel. This mountain will destroy in the same sense that Daniel's abomination will cause great desolation or destruction. Jesus tells us that when this image appears,

Mark 13:19-20

"...those will be days of distress unequaled from the beginning, when God created the world, until now – and **never to be equaled again**."

VII. *The Desolation Reversed!*

Last, and most powerful of all, the curse put forth by God through Jeremiah against the mountain of Babel is *desolation*! The destruction of the mountain is to be like a fiery cremation, and Jeremiah informs us that the burned-out mountain of Babel will remain "desolate" forever.

Jer 51:25, 26

"I am against you, O **destroying mountain**, you who destroy the whole earth...No rock will be taken from you for a cornerstone, nor any stone for a foundation, for you will be **desolate** forever," declares the LORD.

Jeremiah uses the same word to describe the judgment against the destroying mountain that Daniel uses to describe the effect of the abomination in the first place, "desolation." The Hebrew word in Jeremiah's passage for desolation is **shamem**, the precise word that Daniel uses for the "desolation" caused by the abomination. We are led to conclude that:

The mighty mountain (or abomination) that causes *desolation* will in turn be rendered *desolate*!

God will counter the purposes of the kingdom of darkness by bringing its own evil and destructive work back on its head. Zechariah's mountain will be leveled, and this destruction will be a *greater desolation* than that caused by the abomination itself. This will be God's judgment against the abomination, the idol that represents the throne and seat of power for the coming false messiah.

In Summary

The mighty mountain that represents the worldwide kingdom of Babel in the last days will become a physical reality, to be erected in Jerusalem. The pinnacle or summit of this abomination will be a throne, the corrupt, counterfeit image of the throne of God in heaven. This seat of power will be set up in Jerusalem, and will be a Satanic version of what appeared on the Ark of the Covenant. It will also be a man-made mountain modeled after the original Tower of Babel. The pinnacle will be a physical idol which the nations of the earth will be required to worship. It will also be the image of the antichrist himself, Gog as the prince of the capstone, and Horus the "all-seeing god." The Pharaoh of the last days will reign as the *physical capstone*, just as his father, Osiris or Lucifer, will claim to reign as the *spiritual capstone* in the heavenly realm.

Incredibly, this image already appears on the Great Seal and the currency of the United States! It is the pyramid capped by the capstone, bathed in light and adorned with the all-seeing eye of Horus. Under the direction of Franklin D. Roosevelt, this image was taken from the Great Seal and placed on the back of the United States' basic monetary unit, the dollar bill in 1935. As a result, the image that will become the greatest of all abominations has already been released, and not just to America but to every country that does business with America. To understand the magnitude of the familiarity with this image, there are currently over seven billion one dollar notes in float,[42] more than there are people on earth!

Notice as well that this image has been subtly prophesized as the coming abomination by Scripture, *and* it has been prophesized as the throne of the coming messiah by the elite of spiritual Babel, according to the Great Seal. Both the kingdom of God and the kingdom of Satan seem to agree on this matter! Prophecies from both *align on this one symbol*. If you don't believe Scripture, look at the Great Seal. If you don't believe the Great Seal, then look to Scripture.

The Abomination That Causes Desolation

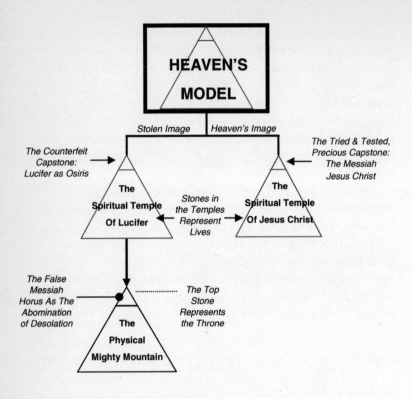

The Abomination that Causes Desolation will be the Recreation of the Throne of God on Earth, and the New Age Tower of Babel

17

THE MARK

The concept of global corporate branding is a new phenomenon to mankind. The same consumer goods are now available anywhere on earth, and this creates a shared consumer experience across large swaths of the roughly six billion people that inhabit this planet. Products are placed into local cultures, not with a single language but with a universal corporate symbol, or seal. The graphic designers and marketers of the Fortune 500 companies have led the way to a form of universal language among consumers globally.

This is partly why corporations attach great value to the intellectual property contained in their symbols and branding. Likewise, it is why they make use of these symbols throughout all aspects of the company's operation, internally and externally. Such symbols appear on products, corporate stationery, business cards, invoices, websites, as well as in domestic and international advertising campaigns.

Biblical prophecy announces the coming of a one-world government. This unified kingdom of man will be like a global corporation. All the powerful techniques currently employed by the Fortune 500 companies in marketing a product globally will be applied to marketing the world ruler and his system of government. The symbols of this world regime will be statements of authority and communal good, and these images will create cohesion among peoples in every corner of the earth. How else would one expect to sell the world on a single product, except through the promotion and maintenance of a global brand?

This thought represents the starting point in understanding the nature of the "mark of the Beast" mentioned in the Book of Revelation. This infamous insignia will be part of a single, global brand expressed through the various operations of the coming world government.

We have already noted that the central image of the reign of the false messiah will be what Daniel refers to as "the abomination of desolation," which has been shown to be the form of a capstone bathed in light with an all-seeing eye. This is the image of the stolen throne of God in heaven, and the image formed by the wings of the Cherubim on the Ark of the Covenant, the throne of God on earth. With minor adjustments, the same symbol could serve as the antichrist's mark.

There are a number of nagging reasons why the mark of the antichrist may be directly related to the all-seeing capstone of light mentioned above.

The Placement of the Mark

First, there is something fascinating revealed in Scripture about the positioning of this mark. We are told it will be found on the forehead or on the right hand.

Rev 13:16

He also forced everyone, small and great, rich and poor, free and slave, to receive **a mark on his right hand or on his forehead**...

This, it turns out, is very specific prophetic information. Beyond mere coincidence, these two locations are precisely where the symbol of the all-seeing eye is placed in the world of the occult. The "eye of Horus" appears on the *forehead* and it appears on the palm of the upraised *hand*, often the right hand specifically.

On the forehead, it represents man's "third eye," his spiritual eye that has been awakened through some form of initiation. On the right palm, it represents the will of the supreme being set in action by the initiate of the Mysteries. To "see" with this third eye, and to act out the will of the supreme deity through human hands, it is necessary in the theology of Babel to proceed through the rites of initiation.

Initiation into the End-Time Mysteries

Initiation has always been the common denominator among members of the elite world of spiritual Babel. A time is approaching when men, women, and children will be led through a form of initiation into the previously secret, but soon-to-be public, occult rites of Babel. These rites may be watered-down so as to be palatable, as they are in the lower levels of membership in the Mystery Schools. However, these initiatory rites will involve a death and resurrection ceremony in which the populations of the world will be symbolically "birthed" into false gods. This initiation will coincide with the receiving of the mark, the sign of the great overseer of the world of Babel, the evil chief shepherd of the flock.

Ironically, the initiation into Babel's mysteries is what denies man the presence of God and His Son. We saw this before in connection to the Osirian "secret rites in temples." As Paul says in Corinthians, "What fellowship can light have with darkness?" In addition, the capstone is the stolen image of God's throne, and it will be used as an idol for worship. This is why Scripture tells us,

Rev 14:9-10
"If anyone **worships the beast** and **his image** and **receives his mark** on the forehead or on the hand, he, too, will drink of the wine of God's fury, which has been poured full strength into the cup of his wrath."

To wear the capstone of the antichrist as a tattoo or an emblem will lead to *exclusion* from the salvation of Jesus Christ. How so? The symbol on the forehead or right palm will be a sign of submission to the counterfeit messiah, and to his corrupt wisdom that says that he is the true son of God. Simply put, man will not be able to serve two messiahs! Jesus makes this point clear when He says "No one can serve two masters" (Matt 6:24). The mark itself will be a form of worship of the false messiah and will represent man enthroned as God.

The Historical Roots of the Mark in Scripture

The symbol at the center of the capstone bathed in light is the "all-seeing" spiritual eye of man. Where does this symbol fit into Biblical history? It originates in the very first encounter between man and evil, in the Garden of Eden. This is where the serpent, Satan, enticed the first man and woman to eat of the fruit of the tree.

The tree was referred to as the "knowledge of good and evil." The significance of this name is better understood when we realize that Adam and Eve already had the knowledge of good; they were in direct communion with their loving Creator in His Garden. As such, they already fellowshipped with the perfect and complete "good." Rather, the type of knowledge gained through the fruit was evil, and was man's first taste of the corrupt wisdom of Lucifer.

For this reason, this fruit was incredibly symbolic. Eating it represented an act of rebellion. The Book of Genesis tells us that this one act "opened the eyes" of Adam and Eve.

Gen 3:6-7
Then the **eyes** of both of them **were opened**...

Were they blind up to then? Certainly not. **Rather, the act of eating the fruit opened their *spiritual eyes* to the corrupted wisdom and influence of Lucifer, as well as to his false enlightenment.** And so the entire human race fell from grace, through rebellion.

It is striking, then, to imagine that the mark of the end-time kingdom of the antichrist would represent *the original sin*, placed on the foreheads or palms of the world's population! The end-time symbol of unity in the kingdom of Babel would point back to the very first act of evil in the human race. This is when the spiritual eye of man first opened to the false light of Lucifer.

To Buy or Sell

Furthermore, we are told that the means of enforcing the receipt of the mark will be the global dependency on it to buy or sell. Anyone who refuses this image of the false messiah will not be able to buy food or engage in any of the other daily transactions that constitute the bare necessities of life.

Rev 13:16-17

...no one could **buy or sell** unless he had the mark...

Again, we are given fascinating prophetic information. The symbol is tied to a person's ability to buy and sell. Where do we find this image today? It is engraved on the Great Seal of the United States which has been placed on the back of the dollar! It appears on the currency of the world's only global superpower, and the commercial center with which all countries of the world do business. That is, the symbol is *already* **tied to the ability to buy and sell.**

The technology to connect this mark with commerce exists, for the most part, today. The symbol or mark will most likely be placed over implanted microchip technology. This kind of micro-technology is already being used, for instance, to identify pets in America. In select cases, it is also being used to store varied personal identification just below the skin of adults and children. Combined with the capabilities of Global Positioning Satellite (GPS) networks, bar code scanning, unheard of storage capacity in databases, and the power of supercomputers, we begin to see that the pieces necessary to confirm this prophecy are gradually being set in place.

Name and Number

We are told that the mark is related to the name or the number of the beast. The derivation of this facet of the mark has always been a matter of debate among students of prophecy. One might be able to make the argument that the all-seeing eye as the mark would link the antichrist to his historical name, the Pharaoh Horus as the son of Osiris. That is, the mark would be "the sign of Horus." One might also, through the link between Saturn and Osiris, be able to demonstrate the derivation of the name Saturn or SATR as "666" in Babylonian numerology.[43] However, the debate over the meaning of the false messiah's name, his number, and his capstone will be left open for the time being.

In Summary

The conclusion is that a *single symbol*, with minor artistic variations, would represent a global brand or "trade-mark" in the kingdom of Babel of the last days. It will therefore be applied in a number of ways. First, the false messiah will have a distinct symbol that will be "his image." Second, he will develop a related "mark" for use in trade. Third, his forces will set up "an idol" as the abomination that causes desolation in Jerusalem. Fourth, the same branded image will most likely appear on the various government documentation, public communications, advertisements and websites.

And finally, it may even be raised as an idol in city centers across the world, just as the capstones on obelisks are today.

PART
IV

THE
MESSIANIC
CAPSTONE

18

The Three Statements of Peter

Having solved the overall mystery of the capstone as an image of the Messiah and His throne, a number of detailed questions arise with regard to the terminology and meaning surrounding it. There is much to be gleaned from more than five thousand years of prophecy!

By carefully working through the layers of meaning behind the Scriptural references to the Stone, deeper prophetic messages can be discovered. One of these messages includes a warning for all mankind.

The Significant Difference Between Stones

The terminology used in Scripture is important. A subtle variation in words can lead to critical variation in meaning, and often these variations encourage us to compare and contrast. The messianic Stone is one such example. The numerous references to this living Stone, and the variations therein, unlock the purpose of its *dual nature*. To demonstrate this, I refer to one of the original passages from Isaiah.

In the King James Version, Isaiah tells us:

Isa 28:16
Behold, I lay in Zion for a foundation a stone, a tried stone, a precious corner stone... (KJV)

In transliterated Hebrew it reads:

Isaiah 28:16
Laakeen koh 'aamar 'Adonaay Yahweh Hiniy
yoceed b$^{\underline{a}}$-Tsiyown 'aaben 'eben *bochan pinat yiqrat*
muwcaad muwcaad...

We are told that the Lord has laid a stone in Zion for a *foundation* (yoceed), and this stone is *tried* and *tested* (bochan), *precious* (yiqrat), and *chief* or *pinnacle* (pinat).

At the beginning of the statement, we read that the Lord is "laying" a stone in Zion. This is a **yoceed stone**, or a foundation stone. This is the stone that forms part of the foundation of a building, often at the base of the threshold or doorway. Symbolically, this stone represents the entire foundation.

By the end of the passage, however, we are told that this stone has changed; it becomes chief or pinnacle. This is the **pinat stone** (or *pinnah* stone). Its English equivalent, the "pinnacle," is defined as "a tall, pointed formation, such as a mountain peak," and "the highest point; summit; acme."[44]

Isaiah has just presented us with a mystery. How can one stone be two different things, and reside in two different places? In other words, how can one stone have two different architectural roles, one at the bottom and one at the top?

To make matters more confusing, a stone at a building's foundation is often referred to as a *cornerstone*. This stone held an important place in the hearts and minds of the builders and the future occupants: it represented the integrity of the outer structure and the spiritual health of the future inhabitants.

"Laying the cornerstone" is still a major event in many building projects. This custom or rite has been handed down through the ages, and is often accompanied with a celebration. In western civilization, the occasion is marked with a ribbon-cutting ceremony, or with a symbolic ground-breaking ritual. The ribbon is often red, symbolic of the sacrifices that took place in ancient times.[45] In the ancient lands of Asia and the Middle East, there was often an animal sacrifice made on the foundation of a building, as a form of a covenant with a deity. Even today, in a number of Middle Eastern and Central Asian countries, a goat or lamb is sacrificed at the laying of a foundation stone.

As is the case with other references to the stones in Scripture, this passage from Isaiah contains a mix of rich building terminology. In addition, the English translation of the underlying Hebrew words creates little distinction, if any, between the two stones. It is therefore obvious why the revelation of the capstone and the solution to its mystery has been veiled for so many years. Simply put, Isaiah's *cornerstone* has been equated with the *yoceed stone* while in fact it applies to the *pinnah stone!*

Clearly, in Isaiah we are presented with two different stones, as follows:

- The **Yoceed Stone**, or foundation stone

- The **Pinnah Stone**, or the pinnacle stone

Throughout the Old Testament, passages that present these two stones blend together their meaning and function. This blending occurs in the same sense that Zechariah and other prophets combine the work of the Messiah at His first and second comings. In addition, the sharpness of Hebrew words becomes clouded and vague when translated into English (i.e. capstone, cornerstone, and chief cornerstone). Thus the capstone has been hidden in both the fog of building terminology and in the less descriptive English translations of rich Hebrew words.

However, the critical message of salvation has never been lost. The foundation (**yoceed**) stone, and its significance, has not been missed over the last two thousand years. The sacrificial death and shed blood of Jesus Christ on the cross has always been understood to be the foundation of the Church, and the source of salvation through grace. This message of the gospel has been ever present through the history of the Church; it is the image and underlying message of the foundation stone. Through the laying of this stone at the Messiah's death on the cross, all of us can enter into eternal fellowship with God in a new Holiest of Holies; we can enter through the doorway of salvation; and all of us can "reserve a place" as a living stone in the temple of Zerub-Babel.

The second stone, the pinnacle, applies more specifically to the end of the age, and focuses our attention on the future work of Jesus Christ. The fact that the pinnacle stone is being unveiled today, in our times, implies that the return of the Messiah is a message of high priority for God and His Son.

Akrogooniaíou,
The Stone in Question

After identifying the presence of two stones in Isaiah, we next turn to Peter, who draws his material directly from Isaiah's passage above. In doing so he reveals more about the various kinds of stones on display.

Peter uses specific words in Greek to reveal key truths, in the same way Isaiah chose specific words in Hebrew. However, prior to analyzing his words, we must first re-read what Paul has to say in Ephesians. There is an ambiguity to spot.

Eph 2:19-22

"Consequently, you are no longer foreigners and aliens, but fellow citizens with God's people and members of God's household...with Christ Jesus himself as the **chief cornerstone** [*akrogooniaíou*]. In him the whole building is joined together and rises to become a holy temple in the Lord. And in him you too are being built together to become a dwelling in which God lives by his Spirit."

Paul refers to Jesus here as the "chief cornerstone." The word for this stone in the Greek text is **akrogooniaíou**. As mentioned before, it is constructed of two separate root words, **akron** and **gonia**. The first is defined as "the extreme end, or top most, or utmost." Isaiah presents the Hebrew word **pinnah**, and Paul uses the Greek word **akron**. When

akron and **gonia** are combined, they convey the concept of the utmost, extreme, or highest cornerstone. In Ephesians 2:20 above, both the King James Version and the NIV refer to this stone as the *chief cornerstone*.

Peter also uses the Greek word **akrogooniaíou** to describe this stone. His words, in the King James Version, are below:

1 Peter 2:6
Behold, I lay in Sion a **chief corner stone** [*akrogooniaíou*], elect, precious: and he that believeth on him shall not be confounded. (KJV)

And, as you would expect, the King James Version translates this word the same for Peter as it did for Paul in Ephesians; both Paul and Peter refer to the *chief cornerstone*. Because both Peter and Paul use the same word, **akrogooniaíou,** it is natural to apply the same English translation to both. However, the surprise occurs when we read the NIV version of Peter. In the NIV translation, the translation of Peter's stone is less specific, and it is described simply as the "cornerstone."

1 Peter 2:6
"See, I lay a stone in Zion, a chosen and precious **cornerstone** [*akrogooniaíou*]..."

The same Greek words, in two passages, have variations in their translations. The comparison of the terminology behind the two passages is summarized below:

	Eph. 2:20	1 Pe 2:6
KJV	chief corner stone	chief corner stone
NIV	chief cornerstone	cornerstone

The Use of *Akrogooniaíou* by Peter and Paul

It is surprising to find that the NIV translation of 1 Peter is a less complete version of this Greek word **akrogooniaíou,** as found in the King James Version. Yet both versions of the Bible render the word as "chief cornerstone" in Paul's passage from Ephesians above. This is another reason why confusion abounds. In Peter's passage, the King James Version is clear, the NIV is less clear on this matter.

This is why the quote from 1 Peter below contains an adjustment to the text, to bring it into line with Paul in Ephesians, and with the true meaning of **akrogooniaíou**. Referring to the stone as the "Chief Cornerstone" may help draw out the distinction between the foundation stone and the chief pinnacle stone.

Peter's Statements of Contrast

In its adjusted form, the revelatory text from Peter reads as follows. Regarding the chief cornerstone:

1 Peter 2:6-8

6 For in Scripture it says:

"See, I lay a stone in Zion,
a chosen and precious *CHIEF cornerstone*,
and the one who trusts in him
will never be put to shame."

7 Now to you who believe, this stone is precious.
But to those who do not believe,

"The stone the builders rejected
has become the *capstone*"

8 And

"A stone that causes men to stumble
and a rock that makes them fall."

With this seemingly trivial adjustment, we find a key to unlock the meaning behind these verses. *Peter has just presented three contrasting statements.* These three statements act as pairs of intertwined, logically connected, and directly contrasted ideas, and they reveal *two types* of stones. I have isolated the three statements as follows:

Statement of Contrast #1
A. I lay a stone Zion (*yoceed*)
B. A chosen and precious chief cornerstone (*pinnah*)

Statement of Contrast #2
A. The stone the builders rejected
B. Has become the capstone

Statement of Contrast #3
A. A stone that causes men to stumble
B. And a rock that makes them fall

Simply stated, all the "A" statements above refer to *one* stone; all the "B" statements refer to the *other* stone. More specifically, the three "A" statements refer to the foundation stone, Isaiah's **yoceed** stone, otherwise noted as the "foundational cornerstone." The three "B" statements refer to the capstone, Isaiah's **pinnah** stone, or the chief, pinnacle cornerstone. And all these statements of Peter contribute to our understanding of the dual nature of the Messiah, Jesus Christ.

In the "A" verses, the stone is at the base or foundation of the building. This is why, in Statement #3, the stone causes men to "stumble." It must be on the ground to catch man's foot! In fact, the verb used as "I *lay* a stone in Zion" in Peter's first statement is **tithemi** and means to *sink down*, and *to settle*. It also means to *kneel down* as in an act of submission.

In the "B" verses, however, this stone has gone through a transformation. It is mysteriously and miraculously raised from a foundation stone to become the highest stone of all. It is described as the *chief cornerstone* (**akrogooniaíou**) in Statement #1, and the *capstone* (**kephale**) in Statement #2.

How this stone moves from the bottom to the top is the crux of the mystery. Scripture has presented us with a riddle, because of the two functions and locations of the Messiah's stone in the spiritual temple being built. One stone is at the bottom, and one stone is at the top.

The answer, however, is close because in Jesus we find a *dual nature*.

The First Coming of the Messiah

At the time of the appearance of the Son of Man on earth two thousand years ago, there was a great outcry among the religious leaders of Israelites. Why? The chosen people rejected the premise that God would send their long-awaited Messiah in the form of a humble, lower-class resident of Nazareth ("Nazareth! Can anything good come from there?" John 1:46). They rejected the premise that He would enter Jerusalem on a donkey, and that He would spend time with tax gatherers and sinners. They also rejected the idea that God would come to man in the form of a suffering Servant, a sacrificial Lamb. He was a Messiah more concerned with the state of their heart than the state of their nation.

As Isaiah clearly foretold:

Isa 53:2-3

He grew up before him like a tender shoot, and like a root out of dry ground. He had no beauty or majesty to attract us to him, nothing in his appearance that we should desire him. He was **despised and rejected by men**, a man of sorrows, and familiar with suffering. Like one from whom men hide their faces he was despised, and **we esteemed him not**.

Could this apply to the true Messiah of the world? Well, yes *and* no. It most certainly applies to Jesus at the time of His *first coming*, for He came to save us through a criminal's death on the cross. He was the stone that was "despised and rejected by men." In His sacrifice He established a pattern to which we attempt to conform our lives: humility, love, respect, faithfulness, perseverance, compassion, mercy, and sacrifice.

Paul confirms for us that Jesus, as the humble foundation stone, is in fact the foundation of our faith.

1 Cor 3:11

No one can lay any **foundation** other than the one already laid, which is Jesus Christ.

We hear a strong echo of this foundation stone in Jesus' parable of the two builders:

Luke 6:47-48
"He is like a man building a house, who dug down deep and laid the **foundation** on rock. When a flood came, the torrent struck that house but could not shake it, because it was well built."

This foundation stone is humble. It is lowly. It is trampled on. It is kicked and spat on. It is willingly crushed by the burden of our iniquities. As such, it bears the entire weight of the building above, and is partly buried beneath the ground below. As Isaiah confirms,

Isa 53:5
But he was pierced for our transgressions, he was **crushed for our iniquities**; the punishment that brought us peace **was upon him**...

All this represents Jesus' sacrificial death for our salvation, the Messiah as the **Yoceed Stone,** the foundation. Jesus, as the Messiah of the first coming, fulfills all three "A" statements in 1st Peter.

· He is a stone laid by God (as a *yoceed*, a foundation)
· He was rejected by men
· He causes men to stumble

The Second Coming of the Messiah
This image does not, however, apply to the Messiah at His *second coming*. Scripture tells us that Jesus is a Messiah of extremes. He is both man and God. He was both dead and is now alive. He is the sacrificial Lamb and the victorious Lion. He is the Alpha and the Omega, the Beginning and the End. He is the suffering servant and the coming King! He is the Author and also the Finisher of our faith.

The story of the Messiah has two bookends, a beginning and an end. The first is Jesus at His first coming, where at the moment of His death on the cross He cried out "It is finished." (John 19:30). The second bookend is Jesus at the time of the great battle at Armageddon, at His second coming. This is when a loud voice comes from the throne in heaven and proclaims, "It is done!" (Rev. 16:17-18).

Rev 16:16-18

Then they gathered the kings together to the place that in Hebrew is called Armageddon. The seventh angel poured out his bowl into the air, and out of the temple came a loud voice from the throne, saying, **"It is done!"**

At His second coming, Jesus is returning as the conquering King instead of the suffering Servant. He rides a white horse instead of a donkey. He wears many kingly crowns instead of the crown of thorns. He leads the army of the saints into battle and crushes the forces of Babel, instead of offering His cheek to their fists and their blows. He is a Messiah to be feared by all those who oppose Him.

At His second coming, we see the fulfillment of the prophecy in Zechariah's core passage. After the defeat of the mighty mountain, the capstone is presented, followed by great shouts of joy from those who know Him, for He is tried and tested and found to be precious.

Z4:7   "**Then** he will bring out the **capstone** to shouts of 'God bless it! God bless it!'"

This stone, the capstone, applies to Jesus *at His second coming.*

He will be the only stone that is able to complete the temple of the new covenant, whose ground-breaking ceremony took place on the cross in 33 AD. He will be the finishing and crowning stone in God's House when He returns as King over all the earth.

Z4:9   "The hands of Zerubbabel have **laid the foundation of this temple**; his hands will also **complete it**. Then you will know that the LORD Almighty has sent me to you."

Jesus will be the stone that was once dead, but is now raised to eternal life! And so we too may become like Him as eternally alive stones.

1 Peter 2:4-5
As you come to him, the **living Stone** –rejected by men but chosen by God and precious to him– you also, like **living stones**, are being built into a spiritual house...

When He returns, He will be the victorious Capstone on the mountain that represents the central point in the kingdom of God on earth. This crowning stone will serve as a demonstration of the truth behind the name written on His robe and thigh:

KING OF KINGS AND LORD OF LORDS

And this revelation is in agreement with the role of Jesus as the highest Stone, which will be:

Eph 1:10
...to bring all things in heaven and on earth together under **one head**, even Christ.

Paul Summarizes the Two Stones
In Philippians, Paul sums up perfectly the two stones that represent Jesus. He confirms the message of the two stones that we find in the words of Zechariah, Isaiah, Peter and the rest:

Phil 2:5-11
5-8 Your attitude should be the same as that of Christ Jesus: Who, being in very nature God, did not consider equality with God something to be grasped, **but made himself nothing, taking the very nature of a servant**, being made in human likeness. And being found

in appearance as a man, **he humbled himself and became obedient to death—even death on a cross!**

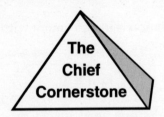

The Foundation Stone

9-11   Therefore **God exalted him to the highest place** and gave him the **name that is above every name**, that at the name of Jesus every knee should bow, in heaven and on earth and under the earth, and every tongue confess that **Jesus Christ is Lord**, to the glory of God the Father.

The
Chief
Cornerstone

And so Jesus at His second coming fulfills all three "B" statements in 1 Peter.

· He is a chosen, precious, and chief stone (the *pinnah* stone)
· He has become the capstone (in heaven, soon to be on earth)
· He causes men to fall

One point remains unclear. How is it that a stone can cause men to fall? What is Peter suggesting in his third statement of contrast? His last statement needs some clarifying.

19

The Stone that Falls
from Heaven

The last statement of contrast needs to be explored. We are in told 1st Peter that the "A" stone, the Foundation Stone, causes men to stumble, while the "B" stone, the Capstone, causes them to fall.

We can see how a foundation stone would cause men to trip and stumble. In vivid imagery, we see Jesus as the humble, lowly stone buried at ground level that catches man's foot as he attempts to ignore Him and the reality that He is the true Messiah. More specifically, by ignoring Jesus and His work at His first coming, man tries to walk in his own righteousness and obtain eternal life in his own strength; *he tries to walk around Jesus.* The point being made is clear: man will always stumble over Jesus when attempting to walk in his own spiritual light or righteousness.

Isa 64:6
All of us have become like one who is unclean,
and **all our righteous acts are like filthy rags**...

Unrepentant man rejects the "foundational premise" that he is a sinner and in need of a Savior. By refusing to acknowledge his sin, and by attempting to build a temple of his own righteousness, man will consistently stumble over the foundation stone that became sin. Jesus, at His first coming, represents an obstacle that no human can talk his way, or walk his way, around.

Jer 6:21
Therefore this is what the LORD says: "I will put **obstacles** before this people."

In this we see the fulfillment of the first part of Peter's third statement of contrast.

Statement of Contrast #3
    A. A stone that causes men to **stumble**
    B. And a rock that makes them fall

But how does the second part of Contrast #3 hold true? How can a capstone cause men *to fall*?

The Stone that Causes Man to Fall
The fall of man can be divided into three main categories: the judgment of men and nations, the toppling of idols, and the ultimate defeat of the head of Babel. Through these three end-time judgments we see the combined fulfillment of Part B of Peter's third statement of contrast.

Statement of Contrast #3
    A. A stone that causes men to stumble
    B. And a rock that makes them **fall**

Because of the prophetic nature of the chief cornerstone, we need to look ahead to the nature and character of Jesus at His *second coming*, and the nature of events when the Messiah returns.

First, we are told that nothing on earth will be able to remain exalted in the presence of Jesus at His second coming. Prideful and rebellious man will be forced to kneel before the Lord Jesus. The worldwide rebellion of the last days will crumble, and rebellious man will be humbled, forever.

Phil 2:9-11
Therefore God exalted him to the highest place
and gave him the name that is above every name,
**that at the name of Jesus every knee should
bow, in heaven and on earth and under the
earth**, and **every tongue confess** that Jesus Christ
is Lord, to the glory of God the Father.

Accordingly, the wicked and rebellious nations of Babel
will be knocked down from their high and exalted places.
They will fall to the ground, and be destroyed.

Jer 51:64
Then say, "So will Babylon [*Babel*] sink to rise
no more because of the disaster I will bring upon
her. **And her people will *fall*.**"

In Babel's place, Jesus (Zerub-Babel) will be exalted over
all the entire earth.

Isa 2:11
The eyes of the **arrogant man will be humbled**
and **the pride of men brought low**; the **LORD
alone will be exalted** in that day.

Second, all the idols of the earth will fall at the appearance
of the Messiah. This makes sense when we realize that idols,
by definition, are exalted objects of worship. They are placed
on raised pedestals in a home or temple in the same manner
they are elevated in man's heart. Every idolatrous thing that
exalts itself in the face of God will topple from its pedestal at
the Lord's second coming. This includes the idols of pagan
deities, as well as idolatrous thoughts in man's heart.

Zech 13:2
"On that day, I will banish the names of the **idols**
from the land, and they will be remembered no
more," declares the LORD Almighty.

As mentioned before, capstones represent false christs. These too are idols. They are elevated, so as to challenge the authority and right of God to rule. The most filthy and detestable of all idols is referred to as the "abomination of desolation." This idol, the antichrist's counterfeit capstone and throne in Jerusalem, will especially be made to fall, hard and fast. It will be destroyed forever.

This leads us to the third type of fall.

Third, the Messiah's return will result in the toppling of the head of the kingdom of Babel. The *true Messiah* will dethrone the *false messiah*: this will be an enormous victory for the kingdom of God. Gog, the prince of the capstone, will fall in the same sense that his abomination will topple in Jerusalem. This is a parallel claim to that of Zechariah, who has told us all along that at the time of the appearance of the victorious capstone, the mighty mountain of spiritual Babel will be leveled, and therefore the counterfeit *ro'sh* will be dethroned.

> **Z4:7**   "What are you, O **mighty mountain**? Before Zerubbabel you will become level ground. Then he will bring out the **capstone** [*ro'sh*] to shouts of 'God bless it! God bless it!'"

The king of Babel, the Pharaoh of the last days, is destined for quite a fall, especially from the exalted position of the counterfeit chief cornerstone.

In this sense, Jeremiah expresses the falling of the counterfeit capstone from a great height when he tells us that the mountain will be like a stone "rolled off a cliff."

> **Jer 51:25-26**
> "I am against you, **O destroying mountain**, you who destroy the whole earth," declares the LORD. "I will stretch out my hand against you, and **roll you off the cliffs**..."

The rug (or temple) will be pulled out from under the prince of this world, Lucifer, and he will be made to fall to the very depths of the bottomless pit, the Abyss. Osiris will be locked away for a thousand years and his counterfeit capstone on earth, the false messiah Horus, will be thrown into the lake of fire.

> ### Rev 20:3
> He [*the angel*] threw him [*the dragon*] **into the Abyss**, and locked and sealed it over him, to keep him from deceiving the nations anymore until the thousand years were ended.

> ### Rev 19:20
> The two of them [*the antichrist & his false prophet*] were thrown alive **into the fiery lake of burning sulfur.**

The evil capstone, the counterfeit chief cornerstone, will be knocked from its exalted throne while the temple underneath him is destroyed. The mighty mountain will be "leveled" and the destroying mountain made "desolate," while the man of the mountain, Gog, is thrown into the lake of fire. This must occur in order for the second capstone, the true Chief Cornerstone, to reign as the sole King of the world.

> Z4:7   "***Then*** he will bring out the capstone to shouts of 'God bless it! God bless it!'"

The Stone that Crushes

In Matthew 21, Jesus makes reference to the mystery of these two stones and their inherent contrast. In His own words on the subject, Jesus, like Peter, creates a contrast:

> ### Matt 21:42-44
> "Have you never read in the Scriptures: 'The stone the builders rejected has become the capstone; the Lord has done this, and it is marvelous in our eyes'? ... **He who falls on this stone will be broken to pieces, but he on whom it falls will be crushed.**"

As with Peter's depiction of the foundation stone and the capstone, Jesus also presents us with the image of *two stones* and a similar contrast. The "A" and "B" stones are the same as the "A" and "B" stones found in Peter! However, the language Jesus uses is even more forceful.

Jesus' Contrast #1
A. The stone the builders rejected
B. Has become the capstone

Jesus' Contrast #2
A. He who falls on this stone will be **broken to pieces**
B. He on whom it falls will be **crushed**

The Pharisees knew that Jesus was referring to them, when He said that those who fall on (or onto) this stone will be "broken to pieces." This is the foundation stone of Zerub-Babel's temple laid at His death on the cross, and it is particularly dangerous to the religious leaders and Pharisees, who lead God's people astray. Their power and might were broken at the time of the Roman campaign against Jerusalem in 70 A.D. Zechariah states that *only by the Holy Spirit* will the kingdom of God be completed, and eternal life for one's soul be gained, not through the power or might (or righteousness) of man. According to Contrast #1, the stone the Pharisees rejected two thousand years ago has instead become "the capstone," the exalted living Stone.

Regarding the "B" portion of Contrast #2, Jesus tells us that He will return to crush the forces of darkness, including all religious leaders in the kingdom of Babel. The King James Version states that this stone will "grind them to powder."

The image of Jesus as a rock that falls from heaven to crush the forces of Satan's kingdom is repeated many times in Biblical prophecy. It was in fact prophesized from the very beginning, in the Garden of Eden, as the end for the serpent.

Gen 3:15
"And I will put enmity between you and the woman, and between your offspring and hers;

he [*the Son of Man*] **will crush your head**, and you will strike his heel."

This is a vision of a fiery, *meteoric capstone* that falls to earth with great force, and smashes and burns everything beneath it. It is a vision that furnishes the interpretation of numerous prophetic references. As an example,

Ps 110:5-6
The Lord is at your right hand; **he will crush kings** on the day of his wrath. He will judge the nations, heaping up the dead and **crushing the rulers of the whole earth**.

The prophet Jeremiah echoes this crushing blow when he refers to the shattered nature of Babel. This blow will cause Babylon (or Babel - בָּבֶל) to become desolate. That is, in a twist of irony, the source of "the abomination that causes desolation" will itself become desolate.

Jer 50:23
"How **broken** and **shattered** is the hammer of the whole earth! How **desolate** is Babylon [*Babel*] among the nations!"

This crushing blow, and the resulting fall of the worldwide rule of man is echoed in Isaiah. Babylon (Babel) is made to sit in the dust on the ground, because the mountainous throne has been pulled out from beneath her. That is, the mighty, destroying mountain and its throne will be leveled, burned up in the cremation fires of Zerub-Babel.

Isa 47:1
"Go down, **sit in the dust**, Virgin Daughter of Babylon; **sit on the ground without a throne**, Daughter of the Babylonians."

This dust-like refuse is the result of the cremation of this defeated, "burned-out" mountain, referred to in Jeremiah.

Themes Related to this Crushing Blow

The idea of a crushing blow from a meteoric Stone from heaven is depicted in a number of ways throughout the words of the prophets. A few are worth mentioning to highlight this point.

One image related to this crushing blow of the capstone is that of the *winepress*, and the rulers of Babel will be the ultimate "grapes of wrath." This is confirmed in the third chapter of Joel. Here the prophet foretold of a great harvest of the nations who have practiced wickedness in the face of the Lord, and who are gathered against Israel in the Valley of Jehoshaphat (a reference to Armageddon).

Joel 3:12-13

'Let the nations be roused; let them advance into the Valley of Jehoshaphat, for there I will sit to judge all the nations on every side. Swing the sickle, for the harvest is ripe. **Come, trample the grapes, for the winepress is full and the vats overflow – so great is their wickedness!**'

As the meteoric capstone descends and pulverizes Babel into dust, so the grapes in the winepress will be smashed. This is also depicted in Revelation.

Rev 14:17-20

"Take your sharp sickle and gather the clusters of grapes from the earth's vine, because its grapes are ripe." **The angel swung his sickle on the earth, gathered its grapes and threw them into the great winepress of God's wrath.**

Another image related to the Stone from heaven is that of *trampling*, the forces of Babel becoming like "ash" and "muddy streets." This is also related to the crushing blow of the capstone at the time of the second coming. In fact, we see this image directly related to the capstone (**pinnah**) in Zechariah.

Zech 10:4-5

From Judah will come the **cornerstone** [*pinnah*]...Together they will be like mighty men **trampling the muddy streets** in battle.

This is echoed by the prophet Micah who proclaims that the Messiah, and those who have maintained their faith in Him, will trample on the wicked as of that "day."

Mal 4:2-3

"Then you will **trample down the wicked**; they will be **ashes under the soles of your feet** on the day when I do these things," says the LORD Almighty.

Finally, the dust and rubble left from this crushing blow is compared to the *chaff or dust* left on a threshing floor at the time of harvest. This chaff is trodden down, and becomes dust-like refuse that will be blown away by the righteous wind of the Holy Spirit. This occurs at a time of "ruthless hordes," echoing again the army of the antichrist at the final battle at Armageddon.

Isa 29:5

But your many enemies will become **like fine dust**, the *ruthless hordes* **like blown chaff.**

The global power structure of Babel in the last days will be crushed, and the rulers will become like chaff blown into the vast expanse of nothingness.

Isa 40:23

He brings **princes to naught** and **reduces the rulers of this world to nothing**... a whirlwind sweeps them away **like chaff.**

Peter refers to the *fall of man*. Jesus refers to the *crushing of man*. Are these two themes presented together, in a single vision of the return of the Messiah?

There is one all-encompassing prophecy regarding the meteoric Stone from heaven, which describes fully the *fall of man* in the last days. Even more, this prophecy specifically refers to a *crushing*, destructive blow caused by a heavenly stone. This one vision combines the prophetic words of both Peter and Jesus! And for this we return to the pages of Daniel.

Daniel's Interpretation of the King's Dream

We have analyzed this passage before, in reference to the stone that is transformed into a great mountain. This time we look closely at the defeat of spiritual Babel, in the form of the statue of man, to learn how it expounds upon Peter's third statement of contrast regarding the *fall* of man, and the words of Jesus regarding the *crushing* effects of this meteoric stone.

The statue in the king's dream, we are told, is a series of earthly kingdoms as if on a timeline, with the first kingdom as the head (Nebuchadnezzar and Babylon), and the final kingdom as the feet (the Antichrist and the end-time kingdom of Babylon or Babel).

Dan 2:31-32
"You looked, O king, and there before you stood a large statue – an enormous, dazzling statue, awesome in appearance."

While the king was observing this marvelous vision, something even more miraculous occurs. A rock is carved out, but not by human hands. As demonstrated before, this is Jesus in His princely form of the exalted capstone.

Dan 2:45
This is the meaning of the vision of the **rock cut out of a mountain**…

This rock is "cut out of a mountain," presumably the sacred mountain in heaven where the Godhead reigns. This rock then falls to earth as the meteoric and heroic Capstone, and crushes the rebellious kingdom of the last days. This end-time kingdom is smashed, or *crushed*.

Dan 2:34
It **struck the statue on its feet** of iron and clay
and *smashed them*.

The end-time kingdom is smashed at the feet of the
statute. This causes the entire statute to come tumbling down.
That is, it *falls*. This is echoed in Daniel's interpretation of
the vision, when he relates the meaning to the king.

Dan 2:44-45
It [the Rock] will **crush all those kingdoms** and
bring them to an end, but it will itself endure
forever.

Notice the incredible fulfillment of prophecy in this
vision. The meteoric capstone descends and *crushes* the rulers
of Babel in the last days, as represented by the feet of the
statue. When this happens, the entire statue of man *falls*. **In
Daniel we have a single stone that causes both the *crushing
of man* and the *fall of man*, at the same time!** This one
account cleverly fulfills both the words of Peter and the
words of Jesus regarding the second type of Stone.

Dan 2:35
Then the iron, the clay, the bronze, the silver and
the gold were **broken to pieces** at the same time
and became like chaff **on a threshing floor** in
the summer. The wind swept them away
without leaving a trace.

As an effect of this crushing blow, the pieces of Babel
become like chaff and dust on the threshing floor, as
described above. The statue collapses into a heap of rubble,
akin to the waste left over on a threshing floor at harvest.
Then the righteous wind of the Holy Spirit sweeps them
away, forever.

The victorious stone, the meteoric capstone from heaven,
will then grow into a mountain that will be an everlasting
kingdom, and a presence that fills the whole earth.

Dan 2:35

But the rock that struck the statue became **a huge mountain** and **filled the whole earth**.

All of these images of falling and crushing relate to the appearance of the Chief Cornerstone, Jesus Christ, the Rock eternal. Upon this great victory, He will become the crown that rests atop the kingdom of God on earth, the summit of the huge mountain that grows from the meteoric capstone in Daniel.

20

THE RIGHTEOUS TOWER

The core passage in Zechariah acts as a guidebook for the events of the second coming of Jesus. Psalm 118 offers an expanded account of the events in Zechariah, events that will take place in Israel during the last days. This amazing Psalm develops themes that comprise the entire Book of Zechariah.

Prior to the Messiah's return, a number of prophecies will have been fulfilled. The final kingdom of Babel will gain dominion over the world, and will create global unity in connection with a new Tower of Babel. The Church will be subjected to intimidation, persecution, and even execution. Israel will realize its mistake of trusting the man of lawlessness, who sets himself up on a throne of a mighty mountain in Jerusalem, as messiah and God of the earth. Because of Israel's rejection of him, the forces of Babel, with Gog as the antichrist, will gather on the plain of Armageddon for one final battle. Jerusalem will be surrounded, its people seemingly cut off.

With this introduction, we can see the outline of the events that follow in Psalm 118. The Messiah has returned to the people of His first covenant.

Ps 118:8-12

All the nations surrounded me, but in the name
of the LORD I cut them off. **They surrounded
me on every side**, but in the name of the LORD
I cut them off. **They swarmed around me like
bees**, but they died out as quickly as burning
thorns; in the name of the LORD I cut them off.

The Psalmist says "all the nations surrounded me," a clue
that something on the level of Armageddon is being
described. This is an indication of the prophetic nature of
the passage, a time of great distress for God's people.
Zechariah, in his twelfth chapter, tells a parallel story.

Zech 12:3

On that day, when **all the nations of the earth
are gathered against her**...

In what is to be the greatest rescue in the history of
mankind, the Messiah will miraculously descend from
heaven and intervene for the sake of His people, the people
of His first covenant. The King will ride triumphantly into
battle on a great white horse, wearing many crowns, and
His saints will form the mighty army dressed in white behind
Him. The greatest battle of all times will commence, as the
world experiences the dawn of a new day.

Joel 2:2

Like **dawn** spreading across the mountains **a
large and mighty army** comes, such as **never was
of old nor ever will be in ages to come.**

The army of saints will follow Jesus into battle, and both
the Messiah and His army will attack the forces of the
antichrist. The description of this heavenly army suggests
that it is to be greatly feared by the evil forces of the satanic
kingdom. At the mere sight of this army, the nations gathered
against Israel will be in anguish, and "every face turns pale."

Fire will go before this heavenly army, and flames will blaze behind it. As the army moves across the land, the earth will shake. The sound of the soldiers' advance will be like the noise of chariots, and they will "leap" over mountains.

This will be the most disciplined and organized army in the history of the world. The soldiers will march in perfect formation, never changing from their course, as an army without fear. As they move forward in rank, they will not jostle against each other; every man marches straight ahead, with absolute focus on the task at hand. They "plunge through defenses without breaking ranks." It is as if every soldier's mind and body will be finely tuned to the goal of destroying the evil and the demonic darkness that plagues the earth.

Best of all, Jesus Christ will be the head of this army, the Commander in Chief, and these "forces beyond number" will be His saints. The result of this onslaught is that the leaders of Babel are crushed by **the Stone that falls from heaven**: Jesus as the resurrected Messiah in meteoric descent, with His army of saints in hot pursuit.

The Messiah Returns

The course of events foretold in Psalm 118 continues with the Jews finally recognizing Jesus as their true Messiah. He "becomes their salvation," both in terms of deliverance from the forces of Babel surrounding them, and more importantly, in terms of their source of eternal life.

Ps 118:13-14

I was pushed back and about to fall, but the LORD helped me. The LORD is my strength and my song; **he has become my salvation**.

Zechariah describes this moment vividly. The people of Israel will weep and mourn when they see Jesus appear, for they will recognize the Messiah that their forefathers crucified. They will remember *the stone that they once rejected*. The Lord will pour on His people a spirit of grace and salvation.

Zech 12:10-12

"And I will pour out on the house of David and the inhabitants of Jerusalem a **spirit of grace** and supplication. They will look on me, **the one they have pierced, and they will mourn for him as one mourns for an only child,** and grieve bitterly for him as one grieves **for a firstborn son.**"

The suggestion here is that the Jews will instantly recognize Jesus, and weep for the "one they have pierced." The prophet Amos reflects on this appearance of Jesus, when he says "I will make that time like mourning for an only son" (Am. 8:10). The Lord, it seems, will bear the marks of His treatment from His first coming, the scars from the nails pressed into His hands and feet, as the Lamb that was slain. The Jewish nation will instantly recognize who their Deliverer is, and they will finally be reconciled to their true Messiah and God.

Ezek 20:40

"...there in the land **the entire house of Israel will serve me**, and there **I will accept them.**"

With this great victory over the spiritual and physical enemies of Israel, Psalm 118 informs us that the children of God will celebrate with shouts of great joy!

Ps 118:15-16

Shouts of joy and victory resound in the tents of the righteous: "The LORD's right hand has done **mighty things**! The LORD's right hand is lifted high; the LORD's right hand has **done mighty things!**"

The Psalmist's "shouts of joy and victory" are the same as Zechariah's "shouts of 'God Bless It!'"

Z4:7   "Then he will bring out the capstone to **shouts of 'God bless it! God bless it!'**"

At the moment of victory, the time of the greatest deliverance in the history of the world, the capstone will appear, representing the exalted state of the Messiah. The presentation of this exalted stone is precisely what the Psalmist next describes:

Ps 118:22-24
The stone the builders rejected has become the **capstone**; the LORD has done this, and **it is marvelous in our eyes**. This is the day the LORD has made; let us rejoice and be glad in it.

Once Jesus has crushed the forces of Babel and thrown Satan into the Abyss for a millennium, the fulfillment of over five thousand years of prophecy will be realized. Jesus will be King on earth, as He is in heaven. This will indeed be "the day the Lord has made," as Psalm 118 says, a promise recorded throughout the whole of human history. The Lord God will have crowned Jesus as the Head of His earthly kingdom, and it will be marvelous in our eyes. Zechariah expresses this in specific words:

Zech 14:9
The LORD will be king **over the whole earth**. On that day there will be one LORD, and **his name the only name**.

With this victory secure, we turn to the final piece of the unraveling mystery behind the capstone.

The Coming Mountain of Zerub-Babel

We have seen references to the original throne of God in heaven, at the utmost heights of the sacred mountain. This is where Jesus reigns alongside the Father today, and where Lucifer was expelled. We have noted that Jesus initially came to earth to begin the construction of a spiritual temple, to lay the foundation as the greater Zerub-Babel. This building effort will end with His return, and the world will rest from its temple-building efforts. This Godly temple – or tower – will represent the central point in the Messiah's kingdom on earth. It will be a true reflection of the sacred mountain and throne of God in heaven.

Following his great fall from grace, Lucifer also began work on a spiritual temple, with his own throne atop a similar pyramidal mountain of stone, a "mighty mountain." In Daniel we learned that, at the time of the reign of the antichrist in Jerusalem, this mighty mountain will become a physical reality, and the Tower of Babel will be rebuilt in the holy city of God as the abomination of desolation. This recreation of the throne of God in Jerusalem will be the ultimate act of rebellion, the greatest of all abominations to God, and will result in the people fleeing from Jerusalem and the surrounding area. The mighty mountain in Zechariah will become a physical reality in Jerusalem, and the spiritual will have a counterpart in the physical. Both the spiritual and physical mountains will be leveled at the return of Jesus Christ.

There has been the suggestion that the Messiah's temple on earth is a spiritual temple or tower, as opposed to a physical House of God. However, a number of prophets in the Old Testament inform us that something dramatic is going to happen in Jerusalem at the reappearance of the Son of God. The landscape of this city is going to miraculously change, it will be forever *transformed*.

A miracle is about to take place.

At the dawn of the day of the Lord's return, there will be such a great demonstration of the Lord's power, kingship, and authority that the whole earth will wonder in amazement. The Psalmist has told us that this demonstration of power will appear "marvelous" in our eyes, and that shouts of joy will resound among the righteous. Zechariah has said that people will rejoice with great shouts of celebration. What exactly is going to occur? Precisely this:

Isa 2:2

In the last days the **mountain of the LORD's temple** will be established as **chief among the mountains**; it will be **raised above the hills,** and all nations will stream to it.

Zerub-Babel's temple will be completed. Its spiritual existence will become a *physical reality*. The worldwide, spiritual temple of Jesus Christ will become "the mountain of the Lord's temple," or more accurately, **the Lord's mountain temple**. It will be a very high mountain indeed. Isaiah informs us that it will be chief among all the mountains of the earth, meaning it will be the *highest point on earth*! Jerusalem, as Zechariah says, will be "raised up."

Zech 14:10

But Jerusalem will be **raised up** and remain in its place...

This will be quite an accomplishment. As noted before, Jerusalem has an average height of just over 2400 feet, whereas Mount Everest stands more than 29,000 feet tall. Two things will take place: Everest will be humbled, along with all other high and lofty mountains, and Jerusalem will be exalted. Isaiah informs us that the mountains of the earth will be "made low" (Is. 40:4). This is consistent with the fact that nothing will be able to exalt itself before the Throne of God, not even the mountains and hills.

The raising of Jerusalem will be the ultimate fulfillment of John the Baptist's cry in the desert, in preparation for the appearance of the Messiah on earth.

Isa 40:3-5

A voice of one calling: "In the desert prepare the way for the LORD; make straight in the wilderness a highway for our God. Every valley shall be raised up, **every mountain and hill made low**; the rough ground shall become level, the rugged places a plain. **And the glory of the LORD will be revealed**, and **all mankind together** *will see it*."

The glory of the Lord will be revealed and all mankind *will see it*. As the Psalmist says prophetically:

Ps 97:5
The **mountains melt like wax** before the LORD,
before the Lord of all the earth.

King David foresaw this awesome sight. He declared that the holy mountain of the Lord will be great, "beautiful in its loftiness." When has it ever been said that Mount Zion in Jerusalem is beautiful for its loftiness? This fact alone is *impossible*, expect according to the great and perfect will of God, in which "the exalted will be brought low and the lowly shall be exalted." Mount Zion will become the joy of the whole earth!

Ps 48:1-2
Great is the LORD, and most worthy of praise,
in the city of our God, **his holy mountain**. It is
beautiful in its loftiness, the **joy of the whole
earth**.

Zechariah has been telling us this all along. The people will rejoice because *they will see* the capstone, the living Stone that will complete the physical Temple Mount(ain) of the Lord.

Z4:7   "Then he will **bring out the capstone** to shouts
of 'God bless it! God bless it!'"

As the stone is brought out and set on high, David envisions God ascending to His exalted throne on Mount Zion. God will "ascend" to the same shouts of joy found in Zechariah, accompanied with the herald of trumpets!

Ps 47:5-6, 8
God has ascended amid shouts of joy, the LORD
amid the sounding of trumpets. Sing praises to
God, sing praises; sing praises to our King, sing
praises…**God is seated on his holy throne**.

The Morning Star will rise at the dawn of this new day, this new glorious age, and will *ascend* to its rightful place in the sky, where He will be enthroned as the Sun of Righteousness. He will rise over the earth and take his rightful place on His throne.

The *righteous* Tower of Zerub-Babel will then unite the entire world under the *true* Messiah and King.

The mountain fortress at the summit will serve as the residence of the King; Jesus' throne will be placed as the crowning stone on the utmost heights. This highest, most exalted place on earth will be the lofty stronghold and seat of power for Jesus Christ. It will also be the pinnacle of the mountain, the Capstone that will complete Zerub-Babel's temple, the Chief Cornerstone of a sacred mountain of stones.

This is what has been confirmed repeatedly by Isaiah, the Psalms, Zechariah, Ezekiel, Peter, Paul, and even Jesus Himself. The Temple Mount will become the Temple Mountain, and Mount Zion will become the *Mountain of Zion*.

> **Z4:9** "The hands of Zerubbabel have laid the foundation of this **temple; his hands will also complete it**. Then you will know that the LORD Almighty has sent me to you."

Zechariah makes it clear in this passage that this mountain is in fact a *temple*. The question arises "will this temple will look more like a mountain or a pyramid?" I suggest both. That the peak of the mountain will be a single "Stone" implies that the entire mountain is in reality a mountain of many stones. This is what Peter has told us in his second chapter:

> **.1 Peter 2:5**
> ...you also, **like living stones**, are being built into **a spiritual house**...

Either way, the mountain will be beautiful in its loftiness, and glorious to behold. One simply cannot imagine the extent of the beauty of this temple – or mountain – because we have nothing on earth with which to compare. We are told that the whole earth will stare in amazement, that it will be beautiful in size or loftiness, and that it will be the joy of the whole earth!

This will be the perfect fulfillment of the prophecy we saw before from the pages of Daniel. The capstone that falls from heaven, in Daniel's vision, becomes a "huge mountain" that fills Jerusalem and the whole earth with its presence.

Dan 2:35
But the rock that struck the statue became a **huge mountain** and **filled the whole earth**.

Ezekiel describes precisely this in a vision of the coming temple of the Lord. After describing the fierce battle of the forces of Gog against Israel at Armageddon, and proclaiming the marvelous day of the Messiah's intervention at His second coming, Ezekiel has a vision of what will happen next. He is taken to a specific place in "the land of Israel." His words confirm exactly what the other prophets have shown us.

Ezek 40:2
In visions of God he took me **to the land of Israel** and **set me on a very high mountain**...

Where in Israel can it currently be said that there is a "very high mountain?" Again, when put in perspective to the tallest mountains on earth, the answer is "nowhere." Ezekiel's whole vision is about the coming of the mountain temple of the Lord. Regarding the summit of the mountain, the prophet is told:

Ezek 43:12
All the surrounding area on top of the mountain will be **most holy**.

Just as the summit of the sacred mountain in heaven is most holy, so too will the utmost heights of this great mountain on earth be holy. At the top will be a mountain fortress; within this fortress will be the Holiest of Holies, where the throne of the King will reside. This will be the seat of world power for Jesus Christ, the living Stone.

Jer 3:16-17
"...**men will no longer say, 'The ark of the covenant** of the LORD.' It will never enter their minds or be remembered; it will not be missed, nor will another one be made. At that time **they will call Jerusalem The Throne of the LORD,** and all nations will gather in Jerusalem to honor the name of the LORD."

The Ark will no longer be necessary because the true Ark and living Stone will be in Jerusalem, alive and in person.

The Nations of Earth Will Visit
When the Messiah's throne is set in place, people from all nations of the earth will come to Jerusalem and worship Him. Jeremiah above informs us that "all nations will gather in Jerusalem." Jesus Christ will be enthroned on high as the light of the world, as the Sun of Righteousness, and kings will come humbly before His throne.

Isa 60:3
Nations will come to your **light,** and **kings to the brightness of your dawn**.

Specifically, the heads of state who have survived will be made to bow to the King of Kings. Zechariah tells us that this will be a yearly journey, or pilgrimage, to the Messiah's earthly seat of power.

Zech 14:16
Then the survivors from all the nations that have attacked Jerusalem **will go up** year after year to worship the King, the LORD Almighty, and to celebrate the Feast of Tabernacles.

The Hebrew word used for the phrase "will go up" is `alah, and means to ascend, as in to climb a mountain. The Lord's throne will be on the top of the exceedingly high mountain that was once the humble Temple Mount in Jerusalem.

This notion of ascent is echoed by the prophet Isaiah. All those who go to Jerusalem, and more specifically to Mount Zion, will have to first climb a high mountain!

Isa 40:9-10
"You who bring good tidings to Zion, **go up on a high mountain**…"

And along those lines, Micah repeats word-for-word what Isaiah has proclaimed so boldly before. The Lord's mountain will be chief among the mountains and all the nations of the earth will stream to it.

Mic 4:1
In the last days the mountain of the LORD's temple will be established as **chief among the mountains**…and **all nations will stream to it.**

The King of Kings will enact law for the whole earth, and will judge between the nations from His lofty stronghold. He will settle disputes and will force mankind to destroy the weapons of war. There will be no war or strife in the kingdom of the Son of God. Isaiah details this for us, and Micah again repeats it.

Isa 2:3-5 & Mic 4:2-3
Many peoples will come and say, "Come, let us go up [`alah] to **the mountain of the LORD**, to **the house** of the God of Jacob. **He will teach us his ways,** so that we may walk in his paths."

The **law will go out from Zion**, the word of the LORD from Jerusalem. He will **judge between the nations** and will **settle disputes** for many peoples. They will beat their swords into plowshares and their spears into pruning hooks. Nation will not take up sword against nation, **nor will they train for war anymore.**

The world will finally experience peace, because the Prince of Peace will have arrived to reign over the earth.

The saints of the kingdom will be like stones in the mountain temple of the Lord; "living stones" according to Peter. And yet, these saints will be co-regents with Christ, and will be responsible for the enactment of His reign. How can both be true?

Our White Stone

Can we, as believers, represent stones in a temple, as well as active administrators of the justice of the kingdom of the earth, as co-regents with Christ? It would seem not. However, we get a hint of the possible solution from the Book of Revelation.

Jesus, we are told, is the Living Stone, and there is a name on this Stone which only He and the Father know. We read this in Zechariah 3:9 and Revelation 19:12. Those who become followers of Jesus are reflections of Him, and as such are also living stones. In Revelation there is a reference to a gift of a white stone with a special name on it, as a form of inheritance to the believers in Christ.

Rev 2:17
"To him who overcomes...I will also give him **a white stone with a new name written on it**, known only to him who receives it."

The suggestion here is that the white stone will represent our place in the temple of the Lord on earth. It will be our mark of acceptance and will be a memorial to us, essentially "holding our place" in the house of God. The millions (or is it billions?) of white stones that will make up his Temple Mountain will be memorials to the saints who are actively administering His reign.

Isaiah presents this thought when he refers to those considered least in the kingdom of man, the eunuchs. Thanks to the mercy and provision of a loving God, the least in the kingdom of man will be among the greatest in the kingdom

of God; they have a name and a memorial better than if they
had sons and daughters.

Isa 56:5
"To them I will give **within my temple** and its
walls a **memorial** and a **name** better than sons
and daughters; I will give them an **everlasting
name** that will not be cut off."

All followers of Jesus Christ will have a name and a
memorial in the mountain temple of the Lord, as members
of the household of God.

The Spiritual Rock
Jesus, the source of eternal life, will return to His people
as the Living Stone. With this in mind, it is fascinating to
learn that a fountain will be opened in Jerusalem at His
return, to cleanse the people from impurity.

Zech 13:1
"On that day a **fountain** will be opened to the
house of David and the inhabitants of Jerusalem,
to cleanse them from sin and impurity."

"On that day," the day of the Messiah's return, a fountain
will appear in Jerusalem. Likewise Joel informs us that a
fountain will flow out of the Lord's House:

Joel 3:18
A **fountain** will flow **out of the LORD's house**...

Zechariah elsewhere explains that a river will flow from
Jerusalem:

Zech 14:8
On that day **living water will flow** out from
Jerusalem...

Jesus will be enthroned at the summit of the glorious
high mountain in Jerusalem. He will be the living Stone. It
follows that the living water will flow directly from His

throne, as He is the source of salvation and eternal life. Here we see reference to the Rock of Horeb, which provided life-sustaining water to the Israelites during their journey in the desert.

Ex 17:6

"I will stand there before you by the **rock at Horeb**. Strike the rock, and **water will come out of it for the people to drink**."

This is explained by Paul in Corinthians, when he refers to the Israelites in the Exodus.

1 Cor 10:3-4

They all ate the same spiritual food and drank the same spiritual drink; **for they drank from the spiritual rock** that accompanied them, **and that rock was Christ**.

The answer to the spiritual thirst of this newly delivered Hebrew nation was Jesus Christ, the spiritual Rock. This was prophetic of the second coming Messiah as well. He will again be the source of deliverance and living water for His people Israel, in His coming Millennial Reign.

The exact meaning behind this fountain flowing from the Rock is highlighted at the end of the Book of Revelation:

Rev 21:6

He said to me: "It is done. I am the Alpha and the Omega, the Beginning and the End. **To him who is thirsty I will give to drink without cost from the spring of the water of life**."

At The Summit

So what, precisely, will appear at the summit of the Mountain of Zion upon the Messiah's return? One idea is presented below.

Similar to His first coming, Jesus will return as the Son of Man, and will be God's presence on earth. He will be perfect in every way, fully divine, yet also in the form of a man; just as He was in His resurrected state prior to His ascension. He will reign as King from His throne within the castle (or fortress) at the summit; this lofty stronghold will be His earthly seat of power.

Enveloping the fortress, as well as the rest of the top of this mountain, will be the Lord's glory, a fiery cloud related to the stone atop the Mercy Seat. This fiery cloud will be in the shape of a perfect capstone and will be the peak of the mountain; **that is, it will be the same image that appeared on the Ark of the Covenant, only on a *much larger scale*!** Previously, when the Temple was established in Jerusalem, the pinnacle stone within the cherubim wings on the Ark was placed at the highest point on the Temple Mount, and served as the symbolic "peak" or "crown." In the case of the Temple Mountain to come, the image at the summit will be the same fiery cloud of divine light, but much grander, because it will serve as a peak or crown for the tallest mountain on earth! It will encase *the entire summit*, and will shine like the sun.

Do we find this vision in Scripture? This thought is suggested in Isaiah, where the prophet describes the coming Mount Zion of the last days:

Isa 4:4-5
Then the LORD **will create over all of Mount Zion** and over those who assemble there a **cloud of smoke** by day and a **glow of flaming fire by night**; over all the glory will be a canopy.

The cloud and the fire of the Lord's glory will return to the summit of the holy mount in Zion, this time the Mountain of Zion. Note as well that the descriptive language of Isaiah seems to link this image to the "pillar" that led the Hebrews thousands of years ago in their exodus from Egypt, and that stood guard protecting them from Pharaoh's army. This was a manifestation of God's glory linked, yet again, to the Ark of the Covenant.

Ex 13:22
Neither the **pillar of cloud** by day nor the **pillar of fire** by night left its place in front of the people.

This cloud-like, fiery image seen during the exodus may have been the same as the cloud-like fiery image that appeared over the Mercy Seat on the Ark. Perhaps the same "pinnacle stone" rested at the top of this pillar by the Red Sea, as a sign to the Hebrews that their God had neither left them nor forsaken them. And so it will be again in the reign of Jesus Christ as King.

In summary, the cloud-like, fiery presence of God will be the intensely brilliant peak of a very high and lofty mountain in Jerusalem.

Conclusion

The temple of Jesus Christ is not finished; there is still work to be done. More than 2,500 years ago, Zechariah cried out to the people of God, telling them to not be afraid, to "let their hands be strong," and to finish the Lord's work. Today, a similar call goes out from heaven to God's people, to fear not, to let our hands be strong, and to finish the temple of Zerub-Babel. This temple lacks precious living stones, and while the harvest is ripe, the laborers are few.

The message and revelation of the **capstone** focus the attention of God's people on the completion of His temple; that is, *His second coming*. Because of this, the revelation of this Stone carries a message to the Church worldwide: **He is coming soon!**

When He does, all war, disease, and strife will vanish before the Prince of Peace, and mankind will finally be united in purpose and in speech under a righteous Tower. The world will then rest from its temple-building efforts.

As the crowning Stone is set in place, God's will for mankind will finally be complete, on earth as it is in heaven:

Eph 1:10
...to bring all things in heaven and on earth together under **one head**, even Christ.

The Completed Will of God, on Earth as it is in Heaven.

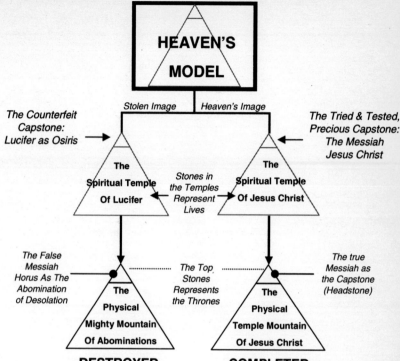

DESTROYED

The culmination of the kingdom of the Antichrist. The rebuilt "mighty mountain" of Babel, with the counterfeit Throne of God at the summit, will be the "Abomination That Causes Desolation." This mountain will be leveled, and the throne destroyed, at the return of Jesus Christ.

COMPLETED

The Meteoric Capstone falls from heaven and destroys the kingdom of the antichrist, leveling the Mighty Mountain. The world then witnesses the coronation ceremony of its new King, Jesus Christ, with the ascension of the bright Morning Star and the Capstone to the highest point on earth. This will be the commencement of the Millennial Reign of Jesus Christ, and will be evidenced by the appearance of the high and lofty Mountain Temple of Zerub-Babel in Jerusalem. The kingdom of God on earth becomes a physical reality, "on earth as in heaven."

EPILOGUE

EPILOGUE:
THE THRONE ROOM OF GOD

The Messiah became a man and appeared the first time so that you and I might personally know His will for us. As the foundation stone, He willingly bore the weight of our infirmities and sorrows. He was willingly crushed for our sin, yours and mine, and in doing so He created a bond between the Father and us. This is a bond so great that it surpasses our human understanding of love. Because of this, we can now enter boldly into the innermost room of God, and stand before His throne of grace and mercy. We can present our needs before Him, and ensure that our hearts are right with the coming King.

Jesus stands at the door of your heart, and gently knocks. He is asking you to let Him in, to begin a relationship that will last a lifetime, in fact an eternity. He wants to invite you into the kingdom and family of God, and to one day reign with Him. He is even willing to reserve a white stone with your name on it, a name known only by God, as an integral part of His kingdom and coming temple.

Today is a day of decision. Choose life! All that is required is a simple prayer. When you walk into His throne room, you become an adopted child of God, and rightfully cry out "Abba, Father!" The King knows who you are, and is waiting for you right now.

The following prayer will help lead you into a direct relationship with Jesus. Pray with me:

Jesus,
I come before You now, proclaiming that You are the Messiah, and that You are a compassionate God, slow to anger, and abounding in love and faithfulness. I acknowledge that my sin is great, but that Your love is far greater. I believe that the price You paid at the cross was sufficient to open a doorway for me to enter into Your kingdom, into Your Holiest of Holies, and into Your throne room of grace. I thank You for this privilege. I also thank You for bearing my grief and my sorrow, and the weight of my iniquity, as the foundation stone. I ask you to forgive me of the errors of my ways, and my regrets, and to make me into a beautiful new creation, a new living stone in Your temple. Thank You for washing me now as white as snow!

I want to reign with You at the end of this age, and to see You high and exalted on Your throne at Your return. I want to be in that celebration, to clap my hands and shout for joy as You ascend to the heights of Your holy mountain, and become the joy of the whole earth. I want to watch, as every knee bows and every tongue confesses that You are Lord of Lord and King of Kings.

Jesus, I choose to walk through that doorway now, as a new child of God. I stand before You, at Your throne of mercy, with nothing to offer You except my love. And I enter now into Your loving embrace.

Congratulations! You can rest assured that Jesus has heard your prayer, and that He is right now by your side. In fact, He says that He will *never* leave you or forsake you (Heb. 13:5). If you prayed this from your heart, *nothing* will be able to separate you from His love (Rom. 8:38).

This is graduation day, and all the hosts of heaven are celebrating for you (Luke 15:7); now you can rejoice, too! The eyes of the Messiah are on you, and they are filled with love.

Continue with me, as we pray for blessing and protection for you in the days ahead.

Now, I ask You Jesus to watch over me, to protect me and guide me, as the Shepherd of my life. I ask You to cover me with the overspreading wings of Your Spirit, that I may find refuge and strength in You. Strengthen me in my innermost being, and lead me into Your Word. Teach me.

I ask You to destroy the mighty mountain before me, to tear down any strongholds, and to dethrone whatever seeks to control or manipulate my life. Jesus, turn that mountain into dust, like chaff on the threshing floor! I ask You to remove each and every obstacle from my path, and make the road before me both level and straight.

I also ask You to equip me with the tools necessary to live as a child in Your kingdom, yet as a light to a world in darkness. For this purpose, fill me now to overflowing with the power and might of Your Holy Spirit. I ask for every great gift that You have for me, and I ask You to teach me a new language, that voice that now unifies Your kingdom here on earth.

To Your name alone I pray.

Amen

Further Reading

A number of exciting topics are covered within this book. If you are interested in learning more, there is a list of suggested reading provided below. All of these books should be available through your local bookstore, or through the Internet at **Impactchristianbooks.com**. You may also contact the address of the publisher for a complete list of titles.

The Healing Ministry of Jesus Christ,
including actual healing testimonies:

Alive Again	Bill Banks
I Believe in Miracles	Kathryn Kuhlman
Jesus Christ, M.D.	David Alsobrook
Overcoming Blocks to Healing	Bill Banks

The Empowerment of the Holy Spirit

Baptism in the Holy Spirit	Derek Prince
Scriptural Outline of the Baptism of the Holy Spirit	G & H Gillies
Handbook On The Holy Spirit	Don Basham
Bible Study: The Holy Spirit & His Gifts	Kenneth Hagin

A New Language

Alive Again	Bill Banks
They Speak With Other Tongues	John Sherrill
21 Reasons Why Christians Should Speak in Tongues	Gordon Lindsay

Also, visit us on the Internet at:
www.Thirdtowerofbabel.com

NOTES

Chapter 2 The Towers of Babel
1   J. Wesley Adams, "Zechariah," in *The Full Life Study Bible NIV* (Grand Rapids: Zondervan Publishing House, 1992), 1370.
2   Alexander Hislop, *The Two Babylons* (New Jersey, Loizeaux Brothers, 1916, 1943, 1959)
3   Refer to R. Laird Harris, Gleason Archer, Jr., Bruce Waltke, eds., *Theological Wordbook of the Old Testament, Vol. I* (Chicago: Moody Press, 1980). Also, the alternative definition "flow away" may be found in *Biblesoft's New Exhaustive Strong's Numbers And Concordance With Expanded Greek-Hebrew Dictionary* (Seattle: Biblesoft and International Bible Translators, Inc., 1994).

Chapter 4 The Temples of God
4   H.C. Trumbull, *The Threshold Covenant* (St. Louis: Impact Christian Books, 2000), 42.

Chapter 5 The Heavenly Throne
5   "Jerusalem," in *The World Book Encyclopedia* (Chicago: World Book Inc., 2002).
6   Uno Holmberg, *The Mythology Of All Races, Volume IV: Finno-Ugric, Siberian*, ed. Canon John Arnott MacCullouch and George Foot Moore (New York: Cooper Square Publishers Inc., 1964), 341.
7   ibid
8   J.A. Black, G. Cunningham, E. Fluckiger-Hawker, E. Robson, and G. Zólyomi, *The Electronic Text Corpus of Sumerian Literature* (http://www-etcsl.orient.ox.ac.uk/), Oxford 1998. Copyright © J.A. Black, G. Cunningham, E. Robson, and G. Zólyomi 1998, 1999, 2000; J.A. Black, G. Cunningham, E. Flückiger-hawker, E. Robson, J. Taylor, and G. Zólyomi 2001. The authors have asserted their moral rights.
9   John R. Hinnells, *Persian Mythology* (New York: Bedrick Books, 1985).
10   Nobert C. Brockman, *Encyclopaedia of Sacred Places*, (Ohio: Marianists of Ohio, Inc., 1997), 185.
11   Colin Wilson, *The Atlas Of Holy Places & Sacred Sites*, (New York: DK Publishing Inc., 1996), 109.

12   ibid., 97.

13   *International Standard Bible Encyclopaedia*, Electronic Database (Seattle: Biblesoft, 1995-1996).

14   *The New Unger's Bible Dictionary* (Chicago: originally published by Moody Press, 1988).

15   Andrew Robert Fausset, *Fausset's Bible Dictionary*, Electronic Database (Seattle: Biblesoft, 1998).

Chapter 6   THE CAPSTONE REVEALED

16   Note: The actual Hebrew words used by Zechariah for capstone are **ro'shan 'eben**, in which the feminine version of **ro'sh** is applied. However, **ro'sh** is used in its masculine form throughout this book in order to reduce the number of variations of Hebrew words.

17   This is an expanded definition based on the original Strong's definition found in *Biblesoft's New Exhaustive Strong's Numbers And Concordance With Expanded Greek-Hebrew Dictionary*. For more information on the Hebrew word **ro'sh**, see Willem A. VanGemeren, ed., *The New International Dictionary of Old Testament Theology and Exegesis, Vol. 2* (Grand Rapids: Zondervan Publishing House, 1997), 1015.

18   "Pinnacle," in *The American Heritage Dictionary, Second College Edition* (Boston: Houghton Mifflin Company, 1991), 942. Reproduced by permission.

Chapter 7   CONFIRMATIONS

19   Israel Ministry of Foreign Affairs, "Jerusalem: Burial Sites and Tombs of the Second Temple Period," Israel Ministry of Foreign Affairs Web page <http://www.mfa.gov.il/mfa/go.asp?MFAH00vb0> (Copyright 1999).

20   Adam Rutherford, *Pyramidology Book I* (Hertfordshire: The Institute of Pyramidology, 1957, 1961, 1967, 1970), 50.

21   The general consensus regarding the symbolism of the Great Seal is that the pyramid is an image of the Great Pyramid of Cheops on the Giza Plateua in Egypt. This is the only pyramid without a capstone in the surrounding area. While this assumption has an element of truth, it misses the ancestory of pyramid-builders in general. The pyramids in Egypt are extensions of the original, post-flood, "mighty mountain" of man. The **original** uncapped pyramid would have been the Tower of Babel.

22   *Biblesoft's New Exhaustive Strong's Numbers And Concordance With Expanded Greek-Hebrew Dictionary.*

23   *Vine's Expository Dictionary Of Biblical Words* (Nashville: Thomas Nelson Publishers, 1985).

24   "Ziggurat," in *The American Heritage Dictionary, Second College Edition* (Boston: Houghton Mifflin Company, 1991), 1406. Reproduced by permission.

25   *International Standard Bible Encyclopaedia*, Electronic Database

Chapter 8 THE RIDDLE OF KANAPH

26   *Biblesoft's New Exhaustive Strong's Numbers And Concordance With Expanded Greek-Hebrew Dictionary*

27   Wyatt Archaeological Research, *The Ark of the Covenant*, Wyatt Museum Web page <http://wyattmuseum.com/ark-of-the-covenant.htm>. Also see Ron Wyatt's research notes, compiled in Ron & Mary Nell Wyatt, *Discoveries Volume* (Spring Hill, TN: Wyatt Archaeological Research, 1993, 1995).

28   ibid. As well, views of the tunnel system and actual excavation may be seen on the video, *Ark Of The Covenant*, available through the Wyatt Museum website.

Chapter 9 THE LIGHT OF THE WORLD

29   The account of the Parker Expedition is recounted in part in Erling Haagensen and Henry Lincoln, *The Templars' Secret Island* (Moreton-in-Marsh: Windrush, 2000; reprint, New York: Barnes & Noble Books, 2002), 95-98.

Chapter 12 FALSE CHRISTS

30   Ninian Smart and Richard D. Hecht, ed., *Sacred Texts Of The World, A Universal Anthology*, (New York: The Crossroad Publishing Company, 1982), 22.

31   ibid., 23.

32   ibid., 24.

Chapter 13 THE SYMBOLS OF PHARAOH

33   The actual capstone from the pyramid of Amenemhat III is in a less prestine shape, showing some signs of its extreme age. Nevertheless, it is surprisingly well intact, and is on display at the Egyptian Museum in Cairo.

34   © Oxford University Press 1969. Reprinted from **The Ancient Egyptian Pyramid Texts** translated into English by R.O. Faulkner (1969) by permission of Oxford University Press, 192.
35   ibid., 145.
36   ibid., 290.
37   See Graham Hancock, *The Fingerprints of the Gods* (New York: Three Rivers Press, 1995), 362. Also refer to Henry Frankfort, *Kingship and the Gods* (Chicago: University of Chicago Press, 1978), 153.

Chapter 14   IN THE WORLD AROUND US
38   Frederick Tupper Saussy, *Rulers of Evil* (New York: HarperCollins Publishers Inc., 1999), 221.
39   ibid., 219.
40   ibid., 217.

Chapter 15   THE STONE OF LAWLESSNESS
41   Louis S. Bauman, *Russian Events In The Light Of Bible Prophecy* (New York: Fleming H. Revell Company, 1942), 24.

Chapter 16   THE DARK SIDE OF KANAPH
42   St. Louis Federal Reserve online report, "An Experiment is Underway," *Monetary Trends*, St. Louis Federal Reserve Web page <http://research.stlouisfed.org/publications/mt/2000/cover2.pdf> (Feb. 2000).

Chapter 17   THE MARK
43   Alexander Hislop, *The Two Babylons* (New Jersey, Loizeaux Brothers, 1916, 1943, 1959), 269.

Chapter 18   THE THREE STATEMENTS OF PETER
44   "Pinnacle," in *The American Heritage Dictionary, Second College Edition* (Boston: Houghton Mifflin Company, 1991), 942. Reproduced by permission.
45   H.C. Trumbull, *The Threshold Covenant* (St. Louis: Impact Christian Books, 2000).

A BLOOD COVENANT
IS THE MOST
SOLEMN, BINDING AGREEMENT POSSIBLE
BETWEEN TWO PARTIES.

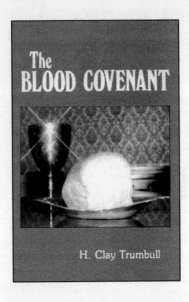

Perhaps one of the least understood, and yet most important and relevant factors necessary for an appreciation of the series of covenants and covenant relationships that our God has chosen to employ in His dealings with man, is the concept of the BLOOD COVENANT!

In this volume which has been "sold out," and "unavailable" for generations, lies truth which has blessed and will continue to bless every pastor, teacher, every serious Christian desiring to "go on with God."

Andrew Murray stated it beautifully years ago, when he said that if we were to but grasp the full knowledge of what God desires to do for us and understood the nature of His promises, it would "make the Covenant the very gate of heaven! May the Holy Spirit give us some vision of its glory."

$12.95 + $2.00 postage and handling

ImpactChristian Books

332 Leffingwell Ave., Suite 101
Kirkwood, MO 63122